Building

Your

High-Powered PC

William Kergroach

1

Table of Contents

1. **Introduction**
   - What is a High-Powered PC?
   - Why Build Your Own PC?
   - Pros and Cons
   - Overview of the Main Steps
2. **Strategies to Optimize Costs Without Compromising Performance**
   - Buying Components on Sale
   - Opting for Used or Refurbished Parts
   - Finding Cheaper Yet High-Performance Alternatives (e.g., Ryzen CPUs vs. Intel)
   - Understanding the Concept of "Best Value for Money"
   - Investing in Key Components (CPU, GPU) While Cutting Costs on Others (Case, Storage)
3. **Understanding PC Components**
   - **The Processor (CPU)**
     - The Importance of Choosing the Right CPU for Overall Performance
     - Comparing   Different

Generations and Models
- How to Identify a CPU with Great Value for Money
- **The Motherboard**
  - Selecting a Compatible Yet Affordable Motherboard
  - Understanding Essential Features and Optional Extras You Can Skip
- **Memory (RAM)**
  - Choosing the Right Capacity and Speed Without Overdoing It
  - Using Alternative Brands Offering Similar Performance at Lower Costs
- **The Graphics Card (GPU)**
  - Comparing GPUs for Intensive Use (Gaming, 3D Modeling)
  - Identifying Price Drops and Second-Hand Alternatives
- **Hard Drive and SSD**
  - Choosing Between SSD and HDD Based on Performance and Price
  - Combining an SSD for the Operating System and an HDD

for Mass Storage
- **The Case**
  - How to Save on the Case Without Sacrificing Ventilation or Compatibility
  - Finding Simple Yet Well-Ventilated Models
- **The Power Supply (PSU)**
  - Accurately Calculating Power Needs to Avoid Overinvestment
  - Choosing Certified Yet Economical PSUs
- **Cooling System**
  - Choosing an Adequate Cooling System Without Going Overboard
  - Comparing Air Cooling vs. Liquid Cooling in Terms of Cost and Efficiency
- **Peripherals and Accessories**
  - Finding High-Performance Yet Affordable Peripherals
  - Reusing Existing Peripherals to Save Money

4. **Preparation: Tools and Workspace**
- List of Necessary Tools

- Preparing a Clean and Safe Workspace
- Safety Considerations (Static Electricity, Precautions)

5. **Step 1: Preparing the Case**

- Illustration: Unpacking and Preparing the Case
- Installing the Motherboard Standoffs
- Cable Management

6. **Step 2: Installing the Processor and RAM on the Motherboard**

- Illustration: How to Install the Processor
- Applying Thermal Paste
- Installing RAM in the Correct Slots

7. **Step 3: Mounting the Motherboard in the Case**

- Illustration: Positioning the Motherboard and Screwing in the Standoffs
- Connecting Basic Cables (Power, Fans)

8. **Step 4: Installing the Cooling System**

- Illustration: Installing Fans or Liquid Cooling

- Airflow Considerations

9. **Step 5: Installing the GPU and Storage**

    - Illustration: Securing the Graphics Card
    - Installing Hard Drives and SSDs

10. **Step 6: Connecting the Power Supply**

    - Illustration: Plugging in All PSU Connectors
    - Verifying Cable Management

11. **Step 7: Checking and Starting the PC**

    - Verifying Connections
    - First Startup and Accessing the BIOS

12. **Operating System Installation**

    - Choosing the OS (Windows, Linux)
    - Creating a Bootable USB Drive
    - Installing Necessary Drivers

13. **Troubleshooting and Advice**

    - What to Do If the PC Doesn't Start?
    - Common Issues and Solutions
    - Additional Resources (Forums, Communities)

14. **Performance Optimization**

- Overclocking the CPU and GPU: A Guide to Boost Performance Without Extra Cost
- Optimizing BIOS and System Settings
- Free Software to Boost Performance

15. **Conclusion**

- Maintaining Your PC
- Upgrading Components
- Tips for Future Improvements

Appendices

- Glossary of Technical Terms
- Final Checklist Before Starting

Introduction

What is a High-Powered PC?

A PC can be considered "high-powered" when it delivers exceptional performance, far surpassing the average standard configurations available on the market. Here are some specific criteria that define a high-powered PC in 2024:

1. **Processor (CPU)**
   - **Type**: High-powered processors are typically top-tier models from leading manufacturers. For example:
     - **Intel**: Core i9-13900K or Core i9-14900K, featuring 16 to 24 cores and clock speeds reaching or exceeding 5.5 GHz in turbo mode.
     - **AMD**: Ryzen 9 7950X or Ryzen 9 7950X3D, with 16 cores/32 threads, optimized for demanding tasks like high-resolution gaming or 3D rendering.
   - **Performance**: These processors are capable of effortlessly handling intensive tasks such as 4K streaming,

high-resolution video editing, and gaming in 4K or 8K at high frame rates.

Graphics Card (GPU)

- **Type**: High-powered graphics cards are those at the top of the current lineup. For example:
  - **NVIDIA**: GeForce RTX 4090, with 24 GB of GDDR6X VRAM, capable of handling 8K gaming and intensive computational tasks such as real-time ray tracing and AI workloads.
  - **AMD**: Radeon RX 7900 XTX, delivering exceptional 4K performance and robust capabilities for creative tasks like rendering and video editing.
- **Performance**: A high-powered GPU can maintain high refresh rates in 4K (120 Hz and above), support multiple high-resolution monitors, and easily execute demanding graphical tasks.

Memory (RAM)

- **Capacity**: A high-powered PC typically features at least 32 GB of RAM, often 64 GB or more for professional users.
- **Type and Speed**: DDR5 RAM with high frequencies (6000 MHz and above) and low latencies is standard for these machines. This configuration ensures smooth multitasking, efficient handling of heavy applications, and support for virtual machine environments.

4. **Storage**

- **Type**: High-powered PCs utilize NVMe SSDs with PCIe 4.0 or even PCIe 5.0 interfaces, offering read/write speeds exceeding 7000 MB/s.
- **Capacity**: These systems typically include several terabytes of SSD storage, often configured in RAID for enhanced performance or increased data security.

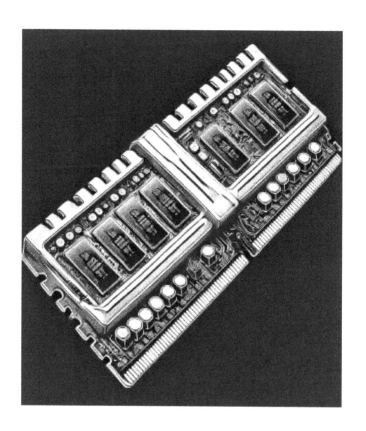

Cooling and Power Supply

- **Cooling**: Custom liquid cooling systems or high-performance All-In-One (AIO) coolers are often used to manage the heat generated by such powerful components, especially during overclocking.

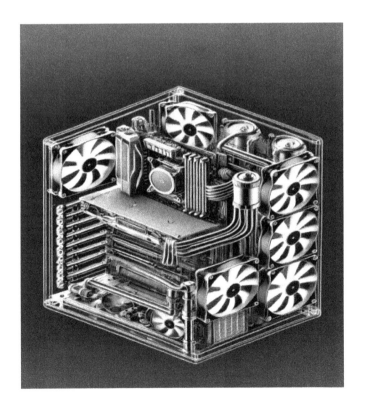

- **Power Supply (PSU)**: A 1000W to 1200W power supply, certified 80 PLUS Gold or Platinum, is common to provide stable power to energy-hungry components.

Éther Features

- **Connectivity**: High-powered motherboards offer PCIe 5.0 slots, multiple USB-C/Thunderbolt 4 ports, and cutting-edge network connectivity with Wi-Fi 6E and a 10 Gb Ethernet port.

- **Monitor**: A display with 4K resolution (or higher), a high refresh rate (144 Hz or more), and support for true HDR (HDR1000) is often paired with these configurations.

Typical Uses of a High-Powered PC

A high-powered PC is designed for extreme tasks:

- **Gaming**: Capable of running all current games in 4K with maximum settings while maintaining high refresh rates.
- **Content Creation**: Perfect for 4K/8K video editing, real-time 3D rendering, and computer-aided design (CAD) applications.
- **Scientific Computing**: Used in professional environments for high-performance computing, machine learning, and complex simulations.

Conclusion

A PC is considered high-powered when it combines the most advanced components available, capable of handling the most demanding tasks without compromising on speed, visual quality, or stability. It's a machine intended for those who require extreme performance for gaming, creation, or intensive scientific work.

Why Build a High-Powered PC?

If you've always dreamed of having a computer that meets your exact needs, whether it's for playing the latest video games, working on creative projects, or simply having a fast and efficient machine, building your own PC can be a very rewarding adventure. It might seem a bit intimidating at first, especially if you're not very familiar with computers, but don't worry: with a little patience and the right guidance, it's entirely doable!

Building your own PC is a bit like assembling a puzzle. You choose each piece based on what you want to do with your computer, and you put them together to get exactly what you want without paying for things you don't need. Plus, by building your own machine, you can often save money compared to buying a pre-built computer from a store, while achieving much higher performance.

The idea here is to show you, step by step, how to create a high-powered PC without spending a fortune. You'll learn how to choose the right components, how to assemble them, and how to make sure everything works perfectly together. And don't worry if you don't know much right now, this guide is designed to walk you through every step, with simple explanations and illustrations to help you understand.

Pros and Cons

Pros:

- **Save Money**: By building your own PC, you can choose parts that offer the best value for money, allowing you to spend your money wisely.
- **Get Exactly What You Want**: You can customize your computer to be exactly the way you want it, choosing the components that meet your specific needs.
- **Learn While Building**: Even if you don't know much at the start, you'll learn a lot by building your PC. These skills will be useful for maintaining and upgrading your system in the future.
- **Pride in DIY**: There's something truly satisfying about using a computer that you've assembled yourself. It's a project you can be proud to have accomplished.

Cons:

- **Time-Consuming**: Building a PC takes

some time, especially if it's your first time. You'll need to be ready to read, understand, and follow the steps carefully.

- **Risk of Errors**: Like any hands-on project, there's always a small risk of making a mistake. But don't worry, this guide is here to help you avoid and fix any issues that might arise.
- **Warranties**: Each component you buy will have its own warranty. This means if something doesn't work, you may have to contact multiple companies to resolve the issue, instead of just one if you had bought a pre-built PC.

Overview of the Main Steps

Building a PC is like following a recipe: you just need to follow the steps one by one. Here's a quick overview of what we'll do together:

1. **Choosing the Components**: We'll start by selecting the parts you'll need. It's like shopping for ingredients before cooking. We'll see how to choose each component, from the processor (the brain of the computer) to the graphics card (for games and videos), to the memory (RAM) and

storage (for saving your files).

2. **Preparing the Workspace**: Before we start assembling, we'll prepare a tidy and secure workspace. You don't need much, just a clean area and a bit of patience.

3. **Assembling the PC**: This is the most exciting step! We'll assemble all the parts like a puzzle, connecting them to create your computer. I'll explain each step in detail, with illustrations to guide you.

4. **Checking Everything Works**: Once everything is in place, we'll turn on the PC to make sure everything is working correctly. If something goes wrong, I'll show you how to fix the small issues that can arise.

5. **Installing the Operating System**: Finally, we'll install the software that will make your PC run, like Windows or another operating system. This is the last step before you can use your new machine!

6. **Optimizing Performance**: Once your PC is up and running, we'll look at how to make it even faster and more efficient with some simple tips.

With this guide, you don't need to be an expert to build a high-powered PC on a budget. Just follow the instructions, take your time, and you'll find that this is a project well within your reach. And on top of that, you'll learn a lot along the way!

2. Strategies to Optimize Costs Without Compromising Performance

When building your own PC, it's possible to get a very powerful machine without spending a fortune. Here are some simple tips to save money while keeping a high-performance PC.

Buying Components on Sale Online stores and specialized shops often offer discounts or sales on computer components. For example, during Black Friday or summer sales, you can find parts like processors or graphics cards at reduced prices. Just keep an eye on these periods to grab some great deals. By buying your components on sale, you save money without sacrificing quality.

Opting for Used or Refurbished Parts Buying used or refurbished components is another way to save. Used components are parts that have already been used but still work perfectly. Refurbished components are parts that have been returned to the manufacturer for repair and testing before being resold at a reduced price. These options allow you to get high-performing parts at a lower cost while staying within your budget.

Looking for Cheaper but High-Performance Alternatives Sometimes, there are cheaper alternatives to certain popular brands or models. For example, AMD Ryzen processors often offer comparable performance to Intel processors but at a more affordable price. Similarly, some lesser-known graphics cards can offer excellent performance at a lower cost. It's about finding the right balance between price and performance.

Understanding the Concept of "Best Value for Money" "Best value for money" means getting the most performance for every dollar spent. This doesn't mean buying the cheapest component, but rather the one that offers the best performance for its price. For example, a processor that costs a little more but is much faster may be a better investment than a cheap processor that quickly becomes outdated. The goal is to maximize performance while staying within your budget.

Investing in Key Components While Cutting Costs on Others To build a powerful PC on a budget, it's important to know where to invest your money. Key components like the processor (CPU) and graphics card (GPU) have a major impact on your computer's performance, so it's worth investing a bit more in them. On the other hand, other elements like the case or hard drive (storage) don't need to be the most expensive for your PC to work well. You can save on these parts without compromising the overall performance of your machine.

By following these strategies, you can build a powerful and reliable PC without going over your budget. It's all about making smart choices and taking the time to compare your options.

3. Understanding PC Components

Building a PC starts with understanding the different parts that make it up. The processor, often called the CPU (Central Processing Unit), is one of the most important components. It's the brain of your computer, executing instructions and managing all the tasks you ask it to do. Here's what you need to know to choose the right processor.

The Processor (CPU)

The Importance of Choosing the Right CPU for Overall Performance

The CPU plays a crucial role in your PC's overall performance. The more powerful it is, the better your computer will handle complex tasks like video editing, playing the latest video games, or multitasking with several applications open at once. If the CPU is too slow or outdated, your computer may struggle, taking longer to execute even simple tasks. This is why choosing a processor that meets your needs is so important.

Comparing Different Generations and Models

Processors come in various generations and models. The two main manufacturers are Intel and AMD. Each new generation of processors is generally faster and more efficient than the previous one. For instance, an Intel Core i7 from the 10th generation is more powerful than a Core i7 from the 8th generation.

In addition to generations, there are different models within each generation. For example, with Intel, you'll find Core i3, Core i5, Core i7, and Core i9, ranging from basic to high-end. Similarly, AMD offers Ryzen 3, Ryzen 5, Ryzen 7, and Ryzen 9.

A newer or higher-end model (like a Core i7 or Ryzen 7) typically offers better performance but also comes at a higher price. If you're on a budget, it might be wise to opt for a previous generation or a mid-range model that still provides good performance at a more affordable price.

How to Identify a CPU with Excellent Value for Money

Here are some simple tips for finding a CPU that offers great value for money:

1. **Check Benchmarks**: Benchmarks are performance tests conducted by experts to compare different processors. You can find these results online. Look for a processor that scores well in the tasks you plan to do (like gaming or creative work) while staying within your budget.
2. **Compare Generations**: Sometimes, buying a processor from the previous generation can be a great deal. It's often cheaper than the latest model but offers very similar performance.
3. **Assess Your Needs**: If you use your PC for simple tasks like web browsing or office work, a mid-range processor (such as an Intel Core i5 or AMD Ryzen 5) will be more than sufficient. For gaming or video editing, a more powerful model will be necessary.
4. **Watch for Promotions**: Processors are often on sale, especially during the launch of new generations. Take advantage of these times to get a higher-performing model at a reduced price.

By choosing a CPU that fits your needs, you ensure that your PC runs smoothly and quickly without spending more than necessary. The processor is truly the heart of your machine, so taking the time to choose it carefully is essential for the success of your PC-building project.

The Motherboard

The Motherboard

The motherboard is the central component of your PC. It connects all other components, such as the processor (CPU), memory (RAM), graphics card (GPU), and storage. Choosing the right motherboard is essential to ensure that all your components work well together. Here's how to select a compatible and budget-friendly motherboard by understanding the essential features and those you can do without.

Selecting a Compatible but Budget-Friendly Motherboard

When choosing a motherboard, the first thing to ensure is that it is compatible with your other components, particularly the processor and RAM.

1. **CPU Compatibility**: Every processor has a specific socket type where it connects to the motherboard. For example, an Intel Core i5 10th generation processor uses an LGA 1200 socket, while an AMD Ryzen 5 uses an AM4 socket. Make sure the motherboard you choose has the correct socket for your processor.

2. **RAM Compatibility**: The motherboard must also be compatible with the memory (RAM) you intend to use. This means it should support the correct type of RAM (such as DDR4 or DDR5) and have enough

slots for the amount of RAM you plan to install.

3. **Motherboard Size and Form Factor**: Motherboards come in various sizes, such as ATX (standard size), Micro-ATX (smaller), and Mini-ITX (very compact). The form factor you choose should be compatible with your case, but larger motherboards typically have more ports and features. Choose the form factor that meets your needs without spending more than necessary.

To find a budget-friendly motherboard, focus on mid-range models that offer the features you need without too many frills. Motherboards from previous generations can also be a good option to save money, as long as they are compatible with your other components.

Understanding Essential Features and Optional Extras You Can Skip

Motherboards come with a multitude of features, but not all are essential for everyone. Here are the main features to consider and those you can skip if you want to save money.

1. **Essential Features**:

- **Number of USB Ports**: Ensure the motherboard has enough USB ports for all your peripherals (mouse, keyboard, external hard drive, etc.).
- **PCIe Slots**: These slots allow you to add cards like the graphics card. For most users, one or two PCIe slots are sufficient.
- **Slots for Hard Drives/SSDs**: The motherboard should have enough connections for the number of hard drives or SSDs you plan to install.
- **Power Connectors**: Make sure the motherboard is compatible with your power supply (PSU) and has the correct connectors for the processor and graphics card.

2. **Optional Extras You Can Skip**:

- **Integrated Wi-Fi**: If you always use a wired Internet connection (Ethernet), you don't need to pay extra for a motherboard with built-in Wi-Fi.
- **RGB LEDs and Lighting**: Some motherboards come with LED lights for aesthetic effects. They look nice

but don't improve your PC's performance. You can save money by choosing a model without these options.

- **Excessive Number of PCIe or SATA Ports**: If you don't plan to add multiple graphics cards or lots of hard drives, a motherboard with a large number of PCIe or SATA ports isn't necessary.
- **High-End Audio**: Unless you're an audiophile or a content creator focused on audio, motherboards with high-end integrated sound cards are not essential. A standard model will suffice for most users.

In summary, when choosing a motherboard, focus on compatibility with your processor and RAM, and ensure it offers the essential features you need. By avoiding unnecessary extras, you can find a powerful and budget-friendly motherboard that perfectly meets your expectations.

Memory (RAM)

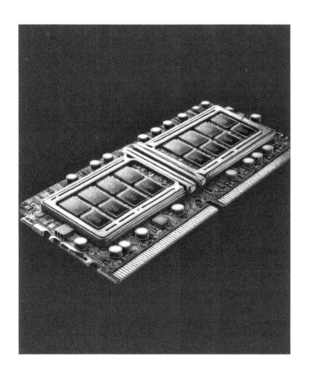

Memory (RAM)

Memory, or RAM (Random Access Memory), is an essential component of your PC. It allows your computer to handle multiple tasks simultaneously and quickly access frequently used data. Choosing the right amount of RAM and an appropriate speed is important for your PC to run smoothly, without spending more than necessary.

Choosing the Right Capacity and Speed Without Excess

1. **RAM Capacity**: The capacity of RAM, measured in gigabytes (GB), determines how many programs and how much data your PC can manage at once. Here are some guidelines to help you choose the right capacity:

   - **8 GB**: Sufficient for basic tasks such as web browsing, office work, and video streaming. This is the minimum recommended for a PC today.
   - **16 GB**: Ideal for gaming, intensive multitasking, and more demanding applications like photo or video editing. This is the recommended amount of RAM for most users.
   - **32 GB or More**: Necessary only if you're doing professional video editing, 3D modeling, or using highly resource-intensive applications. For most users, 16 GB is more than

enough.

In summary, 16 GB of RAM provides a good balance between performance and cost for most users. If you're on a tight budget or have modest needs, 8 GB may suffice, but consider whether your motherboard allows for future RAM upgrades if necessary.

2. **RAM Speed**: The speed of RAM, measured in megahertz (MHz), indicates how quickly data can be read or written. The higher the speed, the better the theoretical performance, but beyond a certain point, the gains may be minimal for everyday use. Here are some tips for choosing the right speed:

- **2400 MHz to 3200 MHz**: For most users, a RAM speed between 2400 and 3200 MHz is sufficient. This is generally the best compromise between performance and cost.

- **3600 MHz and Above**: Primarily useful for high-end gaming or very specific tasks where every millisecond counts. However, it often costs more for relatively modest performance gains in most uses.

In practice, choosing RAM with a speed of 3000 to 3200 MHz will give you a good balance between performance and price. For general use, there's no need to invest in ultra-fast RAM.

Using Alternative Brands Offering Similar Performance at Lower Costs

There are many RAM brands, and the price differences between them can be significant. Well-known brands like Corsair or G.Skill are often more expensive, but that doesn't mean lesser-known alternatives are of lower quality.

1. **Exploring Alternative Brands**:

   - Brands like Crucial, Kingston, Patriot, and TeamGroup offer performance similar to major brands but at more competitive prices.
   - These brands provide reliable RAM modules that are generally compatible with most systems, and they often offer similar warranties to those of more expensive brands.

2. **Comparing Reviews and Tests**:

- Before buying, it's useful to read user reviews and online tests to ensure that the RAM you're considering is well-rated for reliability and performance. Forums and specialized computer websites are good resources for this.

3. **Watching for Promotions**:

- RAM is often on sale, especially during discount periods or when new products are launched. Keeping an eye on these deals can help you get a good brand at a reduced price.

In conclusion, by wisely choosing the capacity and speed of your RAM, and opting for reliable alternative brands, you can achieve excellent performance without overspending. This allows you to maximize your PC's value for money while ensuring that your machine runs smoothly and responsively.

The Graphics Card (GPU)

The Graphics Card (GPU)

The graphics card, or GPU (Graphics Processing Unit), is an essential component for those who want a powerful PC for gaming, 3D modeling, or any other graphically intensive use. It is responsible for rendering images on your screen, and the more powerful it is, the better your PC will handle games and graphically demanding applications smoothly.

Comparing GPUs for Intensive Use (Gaming, 3D Modeling)

GPUs are available in a wide range of performance levels and prices. Here's a guide to help you understand what to look for depending on your specific needs:

1. **Gaming**:

   - **Entry-Level**: If you play light games or slightly older titles, a card like the NVIDIA GTX 1650 or AMD Radeon RX 6500 XT might suffice. These cards are more affordable but can handle 1080p gaming at medium to high settings.
   - **Mid-Range**: For playing modern games in 1080p or even 1440p with high settings, a card like the NVIDIA RTX 3060 or AMD Radeon RX 6600 XT is ideal. These GPUs offer an excellent balance of performance and price for gamers.
   - **High-End**: If you want to play in 4K

or with ultra settings on the latest games, a NVIDIA RTX 3070/3080 or an AMD Radeon RX 6800 XT is recommended. These cards offer top-tier performance, but at a higher price.

2. **3D Modeling and Content Creation**:

- **Mid-Range**: For 3D modeling or light rendering work, cards like the NVIDIA RTX 3060 Ti or AMD Radeon RX 6700 XT are often sufficient. They handle graphic tasks well while being less expensive than high-end models.
- **High-End**: For more complex projects requiring intensive 3D rendering or high-resolution content creation, cards like the NVIDIA RTX 3070/3080 or AMD Radeon RX 6800 XT provide the necessary power for fast and efficient performance.

In summary, the choice of GPU heavily depends on your intended use. For gaming, mid-range to high-end cards offer excellent value for money, while for 3D modeling or content creation, a more powerful card may be necessary for fast and high-quality rendering.

Identifying Price Drops and Used Alternatives

Graphics cards are often the most expensive components in your PC, but there are ways to save money by monitoring price drops and exploring used alternatives.

1. **Monitoring Price Drops**:

   - **Seasonal Promotions**: Periods like Black Friday, summer sales, or year-end holidays often bring discounts on GPUs. By planning your purchase during these times, you can save a significant amount.
   - **New Model Releases**: When new GPU models are launched, previous versions often see price drops. For example, when a new generation of NVIDIA or AMD cards is released, the previous generation models become more affordable while still offering excellent performance.
   - **Online Price Tracking**: Tools like CamelCamelCamel or Keepa allow you to track GPU price trends on sites like Amazon, so you can buy at the best time.

2. **Exploring Used Alternatives**:

- **Secondhand Market**: Sites like eBay, Craigslist, or specialized tech forums often offer used GPUs at reduced prices. Buying a secondhand graphics card can be a great way to get a more powerful model for less. Just ensure the seller is reliable and the card is in good condition.
- **Refurbished Cards**: Some retailers sell refurbished GPUs, which are cards that have been returned to the manufacturer for reconditioning. They are often cheaper than new cards and come with a warranty, which can be a good compromise between price and security.
- **Tips for Buying Used**: When purchasing a used graphics card, always ask for real photos of the card, details about its previous use (e.g., if it was used for mining), and verify that the card hasn't been excessively modified or overclocked.

In conclusion, choosing and purchasing your GPU at the right time can save you a lot of money while getting the performance you need for your intensive graphic tasks. Whether through promotions or exploring the secondhand market, there are many ways to reduce costs without compromising quality.

Hard Drives and SSDs

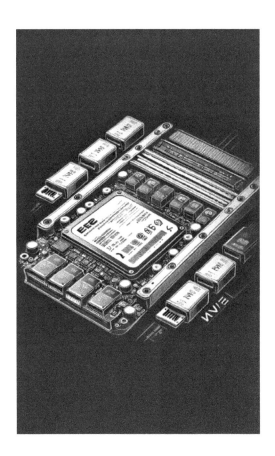

Storage: Hard Drives and SSDs

Storage is a key element of your PC, as it's where all your data is kept: the operating system, software, games, personal files, etc. There are two main types of storage devices: traditional hard drives (HDD) and solid-state drives (SSD). Each has its advantages, and choosing the right one based on your needs can help you balance performance and cost.

Choosing Between SSD and HDD Based on Performance and Price

1. **Hard Drives (HDD)**:

   - **Capacity**: HDDs generally offer large storage capacities at a relatively low price. You can find hard drives with 1 TB (terabyte) or more at very affordable prices. This makes them an excellent choice for storing large amounts of data, such as movies, music, or file archives.
   - **Performance**: In terms of speed, HDDs are slower than SSDs. They use spinning disks to read and write data, which takes more time, especially when loading software or

booting up your PC. They are well-suited for storing files that you don't access frequently but are not ideal for running programs or the operating system.

2. **Solid-State Drives (SSD)**:

- **Capacity**: SSDs are more expensive per gigabyte than HDDs, meaning that for the same price, you get less storage space. However, SSD prices have decreased in recent years, and 500 GB or 1 TB models are now more accessible.
- **Performance**: SSDs are much faster than HDDs. They have no moving parts and use flash memory to store data, which allows them to read and write information much more quickly. This means your PC will boot faster, software will load more quickly, and games or heavy applications will run more smoothly.

In summary, if you need a lot of storage space at minimal cost, HDDs are a good option. But if you want fast performance, especially for booting your computer and loading programs, an SSD is preferable.

Combining SSD for the Operating System and HDD for Mass Storage

To enjoy the benefits of both storage types while managing your budget, a common solution is to use an SSD for the operating system and software, and an HDD for mass data storage.

1. **SSD for the Operating System and Programs**:

   - **Install the Operating System on the SSD**: By installing your operating system (like Windows or Linux) on an SSD, you get a fast startup for your computer. The time it takes to power on your PC and access your programs is significantly reduced.
   - **Programs and Games**: You can also install your most-used software and games on the SSD. This reduces loading times and improves application responsiveness, which is particularly useful for games or creative software that require a lot of resources.

2. **HDD for Mass Storage**:

- **File Storage**: Use the HDD to store large files that you don't access frequently, such as movies, music, photos, or project archives. The HDD offers large capacity at a lower cost, perfect for keeping a lot of data without cluttering your SSD.
- **Backups**: The HDD can also be used to make regular backups of your important data. This allows you to keep a copy of your files securely without taking up the more valuable space on your SSD.

Example Configuration:

- **500 GB to 1 TB SSD**: For the operating system and essential programs.
- **1 TB to 4 TB HDD**: For storing large files and less-used data.

By combining an SSD and an HDD, you take advantage of the strengths of both technologies: the speed of the SSD for everyday use and the large capacity of the HDD for storing all your data at a reduced cost. This approach allows you to have a PC that is both high-performing and economical, optimized for your specific needs.

The Case (Chassis)

The case, or chassis, is an often overlooked but essential component of your PC. It houses all your components and plays a crucial role in ensuring proper cooling, ease of assembly, and future upgrades. Choosing the right case can make your building experience smoother and contribute to the overall performance and longevity of your PC. Here's how to select a case that balances cost, functionality, and aesthetics.

The Case (Chassis)

The case, or chassis, is the shell that houses all your PC components. It plays a crucial role not only in holding your components but also in ensuring proper ventilation to keep your system cool. While cases come in all shapes and sizes, from the simplest to the most sophisticated, you can save money by choosing a model that meets your needs without sacrificing ventilation or compatibility with your other components.

How to Save on the Case Without Sacrificing Ventilation or Compatibility

1. **Focus on the Essentials**:

   - **Size and Compatibility**: Make sure the case is large enough to accommodate your motherboard, graphics card, and other components. Common form factors include ATX, Micro-ATX, and Mini-ITX. If you have a standard ATX motherboard, a classic ATX case will suffice, often at a reasonable cost. Smaller cases (like Mini-ITX) can be more expensive and require specific, more compact components.

51

- **Cable Management**: Good cable management not only keeps the interior tidy but also improves airflow. Opt for a case with basic cable management features, such as openings to route cables behind the motherboard. This is an essential feature but doesn't need to be complex or costly.
- **Connectors and Ports**: A simple case with a few front USB ports and a headphone/microphone jack will be sufficient for most users. More expensive cases often offer more connectors, but these aren't necessary if your motherboard already has these options or if you use an external USB hub.

2. **Avoid Unnecessary Features**:

- **RGB Lighting**: While RGB lighting (colorful illumination) is trendy, it doesn't improve performance. Choosing a case without RGB lighting can save you money without compromising functionality.
- **Tempered Glass Panels**: Tempered

glass panels can be aesthetically pleasing but add to the case's cost. A model with a metal or opaque plastic side panel will work just as well, especially if appearance isn't your priority.

3. **Ensure Good Ventilation**:

- **Basic but Effective Ventilation**: Look for a case with at least one front intake fan and one rear exhaust fan. Some budget cases may only include one fan, but as long as the case has room to add one or two additional fans if needed, it will maintain good airflow.

- **Dust Filters**: A case with removable dust filters (at the front, bottom, and top) is a plus, as they keep dust out and are easy to clean. This extends the life of your components by keeping them clean and reducing the need for maintenance.

Choosing Simple Yet Well-Ventilated Models

1. **Popular Models with Good Value**:

- **Cooler Master MasterBox Q300L**:

A compact but well-designed case with good ventilation and a simple design. It offers ATX and Micro-ATX compatibility and features magnetic dust filters. It's an excellent choice for tight budgets.

- **NZXT H510**: This case offers excellent cable management and decent ventilation without unnecessary features. It has a clean design and is often available at a competitive price.
- **Fractal Design Focus G**: An economical ATX case with two included LED fans. It offers good airflow and a spacious interior for easy component assembly.

2. **Selection Criteria**:

- **Price vs. Functionality**: Look for cases that offer essential features like good ventilation, basic cable management, and enough space for your components without getting lost in aesthetic extras or expensive gadgets.
- **Reviews and Tests**: Before buying,

check user reviews and online tests to ensure the case you choose has a good reputation for build quality, ventilation, and ease of assembly.

You don't need to spend a lot on a case that gets the job done. By focusing on compatibility, ventilation, and basic functionality, you can find a simple, efficient, and affordable case that protects your components and ensures good airflow to keep your PC healthy.

However, a large and well-equipped case is essential for accommodating a powerful configuration, ensuring good ventilation, and allowing for future upgrades. Here are some case models known for their large size, build quality, and advanced features:

1. Fractal Design Meshify 2 XL

- **Size**: Full Tower
- **Features**:
  - **Ventilation**: Designed for optimal airflow with a mesh front, the Meshify 2 XL can accommodate up to 11 fans and is compatible with liquid cooling

radiators up to 420 mm.

- **Interior Space**: Capable of housing motherboards up to E-ATX size, this case offers immense space for large components, including graphics cards up to 520 mm in length.
- **Storage Options**: Can install up to 18 hard drives (HDD) or SSDs thanks to modular drive cages.
- **Cable Management**: The case features well-thought-out cable management with large cable passages and Velcro straps.
- **Connectivity**: Front USB 3.2 Gen 2 Type-C ports, along with USB 3.0 and audio ports.

2. Corsair Obsidian Series 1000D

- **Size**: Super Tower
- **Features**:
  - **Ventilation**: This massive case can support up to 13 fans and liquid cooling radiators up to 480 mm, with advanced airflow management for extreme

configurations.

- **Interior Space**: The Corsair 1000D can accommodate two systems simultaneously (one E-ATX and one Mini-ITX), with enough space for multiple graphics cards and substantial storage.
- **Storage Options**: Can install up to five 3.5-inch hard drives and six 2.5-inch SSDs.
- **Cable Management**: Advanced cable management system with integrated channels and clips for clean assembly.
- **Connectivity**: Front panel with USB 3.1 Type-C, USB 3.0 ports, and RGB lighting control.

3. Lian Li PC-O11 Dynamic XL

- **Size**: Full Tower
- **Features**:
  - **Ventilation**: Designed for liquid cooling with a modular design that can accommodate up to three 360 mm radiators simultaneously. It can also

support up to 10 fans for air cooling.

- **Interior Space**: The Lian Li PC-O11 Dynamic XL supports motherboards up to E-ATX size and can house large graphics cards and complex liquid cooling systems.
- **Storage Options**: Capacity to accommodate up to four 3.5-inch hard drives and six 2.5-inch SSDs.
- **Cable Management**: Excellent cable management system with dedicated space behind the motherboard and a removable cover to hide cables.
- **Connectivity**: Front USB 3.1 Type-C and USB 3.0 ports, with a sleek, modern design in tempered glass.

4. **Phanteks Enthoo Elite**

- **Size**: Super Tower
- **Features**:
  - **Ventilation**: Designed for the most demanding configurations,

the Enthoo Elite supports up to 15 fans and liquid cooling radiators up to 480 mm, with flexible mounting options.

- **Interior Space**: It can accommodate E-ATX and XL-ATX motherboards, multiple graphics cards, and even a dual system (ATX + ITX) with ample space for efficient cooling.
- **Storage Options**: Supports up to 12 3.5-inch hard drives and 12 2.5-inch SSDs.
- **Cable Management**: Excellent cable management system with dedicated channels, Velcro straps, and cable covers for a clean interior.
- **Connectivity**: USB 3.1 Type-C ports, HDMI for VR, integrated RGB lighting controls, and support for a fan hub.

5. Cooler Master Cosmos C700M

- **Size**: Full Tower
- **Features**:
  - **Ventilation**: Supports up to nine

fans and liquid cooling radiators up to 420 mm, with optimized airflow for high-performance configurations.

- **Interior Space**: The Cosmos C700M is designed for flexible configurations with a modular chassis that allows for component reorganization according to your preferences, including E-ATX motherboards.
- **Storage Options**: Can accommodate up to five 3.5-inch hard drives and four 2.5-inch SSDs.
- **Cable Management**: Cable management system with a rear cover and well-positioned cable passages for clean organization.
- **Connectivity**: USB 3.1 Type-C ports, integrated addressable RGB with a control panel, and an iconic design with aluminum handles.

Conclusion

Each of these cases is large and well-equipped, offering excellent ventilation, advanced cable management, and ample space to accommodate high-end configurations. The choice between them will depend on your specific needs in terms of size, design, cooling, and additional features.

Power Supply (PSU)

Power Supply (PSU)

The power supply unit (PSU) is the component that provides the necessary energy to all parts of your PC. Choosing the right power supply is crucial: it must be powerful enough to run your system, but not oversized, which would lead to unnecessary spending. Here's how to calculate the required power accurately and select a certified but economical PSU.

Calculating the Required Power Accurately to Avoid Overspending

1. **Estimate Your System's Power Consumption**: Each component of your PC consumes a certain amount of power, expressed in watts (W). The components that consume the most are typically the processor (CPU) and the graphics card (GPU). Here's a general estimate of the power consumption of the main components:

   - **Processor (CPU)**: Approximately 65W to 125W depending on the model.
   - **Graphics Card (GPU)**: Approximately 150W to 350W for

mid-range to high-end graphics cards.

- **Motherboard and Peripherals (RAM, Hard Drives, etc.)**: Around 50W to 100W.
- **Fans and Cooling System**: Approximately 10W to 30W.

For example, a gaming PC with a mid-range processor and a high-performance graphics card might require around 400W to 500W in total.

2. **Use an Online Power Calculator**: To get a more precise estimate, you can use online power calculators. These tools allow you to enter the specifics of your configuration (CPU model, GPU, number of hard drives, etc.) and automatically calculate the recommended power for your PSU. They usually provide a safety margin to prevent the power supply from running at full capacity all the time.

3. **Add a Safety Margin**: Once you've estimated the necessary power, it's advisable to add a safety margin of about 20% to 30%. For example, if your configuration consumes around 400W, opt for a power supply of at least 500W to

550W. This ensures system stability even during power consumption spikes or if you decide to upgrade your components in the future.

Choosing Certified but Economical PSUs

1. **Understanding Efficiency Certifications**: Power supplies are often rated by their energy efficiency, indicated by certifications like 80 PLUS. This certification means that the power supply efficiently converts energy from your electrical outlet into usable power for your components, with less loss as heat. The certification levels are:

   - **80 PLUS**: 80% efficiency at 20%, 50%, and 100% load.
   - **80 PLUS Bronze**: Slightly better efficiency, around 82% to 85%.
   - **80 PLUS Silver/Gold/Platinum**: These certifications offer even higher efficiencies, up to 90% and above.

   For most users, a PSU certified 80 PLUS Bronze offers a good balance between price and efficiency. Opting for 80 PLUS Gold can be worthwhile if you want to reduce your electricity consumption, but it usually costs a bit more.

2. **Choosing Reliable yet Affordable Brands and Models**:

- **Brands to Consider**: Brands like Corsair, EVGA, Seasonic, and Cooler Master are well-known for their reliable and affordable power supplies. They offer a wide range of models, from entry-level to high-end, with 80 PLUS certifications.
- **Recommended Budget Models**:
  - **Corsair CX550 (550W, 80 PLUS Bronze)**: An excellent choice for a mid-range gaming PC. This model is known for its reliability and affordable price.
  - **EVGA 600 W1 (600W, 80 PLUS White)**: An economical option for those who need a bit more power without breaking the bank.
  - **Seasonic S12III (500W, 80 PLUS Bronze)**: A reliable PSU with good certification and a competitive price.

3. **Avoid Non-Certified or Ultra-Cheap Power Supplies**: While it may be tempting to choose the cheapest possible power supply, it's important not to sacrifice quality. Non-certified or extremely cheap power supplies can be inefficient, unstable, or even dangerous for your components. A good power supply protects your components and ensures stable operation of your PC in the long run.

In Summary

To choose a power supply, first calculate the power you actually need, adding a safety margin, and then opt for a model certified 80 PLUS Bronze or higher from a reputable brand. This will save you money while ensuring your PC runs reliably and efficiently.

Cooling System

Cooling System

The cooling system is crucial for maintaining the temperature of your components, particularly the processor (CPU), at an optimal level. Effective cooling ensures that your PC runs stably, without the risk of overheating, which could damage components or reduce performance. However, it's possible to choose a cooling system that meets your needs without overspending. Here's how to do that, along with a comparison between air and liquid cooling systems.

Choosing an Adequate Cooling System Without Overspending

1. **Assessing Your Needs**:

   - **Normal Use (Office Work, Browsing, Occasional Gaming)**: For standard usage, an air cooling system with a good CPU fan is usually sufficient. These systems are affordable, easy to install, and offer good performance for moderate workloads.

   - **Intensive Use (Gaming, Overclocking, Content Creation)**: If you have a powerful processor or plan to do overclocking (increasing the CPU speed beyond factory specifications), you'll need a more robust cooling system. In this case, a high-quality fan or a liquid cooling system may be necessary.

2. **Avoiding Overinvestment**:

   - It's important to choose a cooling system that matches your configuration without going overboard. For example, if you don't run intensive applications or overclock, a standard air cooler will be more than adequate, even with a powerful CPU.

3. **Recommended Brands and Models**:

- **Air Cooling**:
  - **Cooler Master Hyper 212 EVO**: A classic in air cooling, known for its excellent price-to-performance ratio. It's effective for most mainstream processors.
  - **Noctua NH-U12S**: Slightly more expensive but offers exceptional cooling performance and is very quiet.
- **Liquid Cooling**:
  - **Corsair Hydro Series H60**: An affordable and compact liquid cooler, suitable for smaller configurations or smaller cases.
  - **NZXT Kraken X53**: A popular model for those seeking high-performance liquid cooling, with customization options via RGB lighting.

Comparing Air vs. Liquid Cooling in Terms of

Cost/Efficiency

1. Air Cooling:

- **Cost**: Air cooling is generally less expensive than liquid cooling. CPU fans range from €20 to €60 for the more efficient models, making it an economical option.
- **Efficiency**: For most users, a good air cooler is efficient enough to keep temperatures low, even during prolonged gaming sessions or creative work. Fans are easy to install and maintain, and they are also very reliable.
- **Noise**: Some fans can be noisier, especially under load. However, higher-quality models like those from Noctua are designed to be quiet while providing excellent cooling.

2. Liquid Cooling:

- **Cost**: Liquid cooling is generally more expensive, with models ranging from €60 to €150 or more. It's a bigger investment, but necessary for some high-end configurations.
- **Efficiency**: Liquid cooling is more

efficient at dissipating heat, especially for powerful or overclocked configurations. It can maintain lower temperatures even under heavy loads, allowing your CPU to perform at its best without risk of overheating.

- **Aesthetics and Installation**: Liquid cooling systems are often chosen for their aesthetics, with customization options via RGB LEDs. However, they are more complex to install than air coolers and require occasional maintenance (such as checking liquid levels).
- **Noise**: Liquid cooling systems are generally quieter, as they don't need to spin fans as fast as air cooling systems to achieve the same level of heat dissipation.

Summary:

- **Air Cooling**: Recommended for the majority of users, especially if you don't overclock. It's more economical, easier to install, and offers sufficient efficiency for most tasks.
- **Liquid Cooling**: Recommended for high-

end configurations, overclockers, or those who want a specific aesthetic. While more expensive, it provides better thermal efficiency and is generally quieter.

Conclusion:

The choice between air and liquid cooling depends on your budget, performance needs, and aesthetic preferences. For most users, a good air cooling system is sufficient, while liquid cooling is preferable for high-performance configurations or for those looking for a sleek PC with optimal temperatures.

Peripherals and Accessories

Peripherals and accessories include all the external components you use with your PC, such as the keyboard, mouse, monitor, and speakers. While they aren't directly related to your computer's performance, they play a crucial role in your user experience. Here's how to choose high-performance yet affordable peripherals and how to save by reusing equipment you already own.

Finding High-Performance Yet Affordable

Peripheral Options

1. **Keyboard and Mouse**:
   - When selecting a keyboard and mouse, consider how you'll be using them. For general office work, a basic but reliable set will suffice. Gamers or content creators may want to invest in models with additional features, like programmable keys or higher DPI settings for the mouse.
   - **Recommended Budget Options**:
     - **Logitech K120 (Keyboard)**: A basic, durable keyboard that is comfortable to use and very affordable.
     - **Logitech M510 (Mouse)**: A budget-friendly, wireless mouse that offers good ergonomics and responsive tracking, suitable for general use.
     - **Mechanical Keyboards**: For a more premium feel, consider a budget mechanical keyboard like the **Redragon K552**, which offers the tactile feedback of mechanical keys without

breaking the bank.

The rest of the peripherals such as monitors, speakers, and other accessories will follow a similar approach, balancing between cost-effectiveness and meeting the specific needs of the user.

This approach ensures you're equipped with the tools you need for an enjoyable and efficient computing experience without unnecessary expenditures.

• Peripherals and Accessories

Here are some recommended options for keyboards, mice, and monitors that balance performance with affordability:

Keyboards:

- **Logitech K120**: A simple and reliable wired keyboard, ideal for everyday use. It's affordable, durable, and comfortable for typing, making it perfect for general office tasks or home use.
- **Redragon K552**: An affordable mechanical keyboard for gamers, featuring backlit keys. It offers good responsiveness for gaming while remaining within a reasonable budget, providing the tactile feel that many gamers prefer.

Mice:

- **Logitech M510**: An ergonomic wireless mouse, well-suited for office work and general use, with good battery life. Its comfortable design and reliable performance make it a great choice for those who spend long hours at the computer.

- **Razer DeathAdder Essential**: An affordable and precise wired mouse, highly regarded by gamers for its responsiveness and comfort. It's an excellent choice for gaming or any task requiring precision and speed.

Monitors:

- When choosing a monitor, consider factors such as resolution, refresh rate, and size, based on your specific needs. Here are some options to consider:

1. **Acer R240HY**: A budget-friendly 23.8-inch monitor with a Full HD (1920x1080) resolution, IPS panel for good color accuracy, and wide viewing angles. It's an excellent choice for general use, including office work and multimedia consumption.

2. **Dell S2721HGF**: A 27-inch curved gaming monitor with a Full HD resolution, 144Hz refresh rate, and 1ms response time. It's designed for smooth gameplay and provides an immersive experience at a reasonable price.

3. **ASUS TUF Gaming VG249Q**: A 24-inch monitor with Full HD resolution, 144Hz refresh rate, and FreeSync support, making it ideal for gamers who want a fluid and responsive gaming experience without breaking the bank.

These options provide a good mix of functionality, performance, and cost-effectiveness, ensuring you can build a well-rounded setup that suits your needs without overspending.

- **Monitors:**

- **Acer R240HY**: A 24-inch monitor with Full HD (1080p) resolution, offering solid performance for most uses, including light gaming and office work, at a very competitive price. It's a great all-around monitor for those looking for quality without high costs.

- **Dell SE2419Hx**: Another 24-inch Full HD monitor with good viewing angles and clear image quality, perfect for work and entertainment. It's priced affordably, making it a great option for those needing a reliable monitor for everyday tasks.

Headsets and Speakers:

When choosing audio peripherals, consider whether you need immersive sound for gaming, clear audio for communication, or powerful speakers for music and entertainment.

1. **Headsets**:

   - **Logitech H390**: A budget-friendly, wired USB headset with noise-canceling microphone and comfortable ear pads. It's ideal for office work, video conferencing, and online communication, providing clear audio and voice quality.
   - **HyperX Cloud Stinger**: An affordable gaming headset known for its comfort and good sound quality. It features memory foam ear cushions, a

noise-canceling microphone, and is lightweight, making it a solid choice for long gaming sessions.

2. **Speakers**:

- **Creative Pebble 2.0**: Compact desktop speakers with a modern design and good sound quality, perfect for small spaces. These are great for general use, offering clear audio for music, videos, and light gaming.
- **Logitech Z313**: A 2.1 speaker system with a subwoofer, providing rich sound for music and movies. It's a cost-effective solution for those who want a bit more bass and power in their audio setup without spending too much.

These options provide a balance of quality, performance, and affordability, ensuring you have an enjoyable audio experience whether you're working, gaming, or watching movies.

- **Headsets:**

- **HyperX Cloud Stinger**: An affordable gaming headset with good sound quality and an integrated microphone, making it ideal for gaming and online calls. Its lightweight design and comfortable ear cushions make it great for extended use.
- **Logitech H390**: A USB headset with a noise-canceling microphone, perfect for

online meetings or working from home. It offers clear audio and voice quality, with comfortable ear pads for long sessions.

Speakers:

- **Creative Pebble 2.0**: Compact and affordable desktop speakers with surprisingly good sound for their size, perfect for use on a desk for everyday tasks like listening to music, watching videos, or light gaming.
- **Logitech Z313**: A 2.1 speaker system with a subwoofer, providing enhanced sound quality with rich bass, making it a great value for those looking to improve their audio experience without spending a lot.

Webcams:

When selecting a webcam, consider the resolution, frame rate, and additional features like autofocus or built-in microphones, which can significantly enhance your video conferencing or streaming experience.

1. **Logitech C270**: A budget-friendly 720p HD webcam, ideal for basic video calls. It offers decent video quality for the price,

with a built-in microphone for clear audio.

2. **Logitech C920**: A popular choice for those looking for a step up in video quality, this 1080p Full HD webcam offers excellent clarity and performance for video conferencing, streaming, or recording. It also features autofocus and dual microphones for stereo sound.

3. **Razer Kiyo**: A webcam designed for streamers, featuring 1080p video quality with a built-in ring light to ensure you're well-lit in any environment. It's a great option for those who need high-quality video and lighting in one compact device.

These webcams cater to a range of needs, from basic video calls to high-quality streaming, ensuring you have the right tool for your setup.

Webcams:

- **Logitech C270**: A simple and economical HD webcam, ideal for video calls and online meetings. It provides decent video quality at a budget-friendly price.
- **Microsoft LifeCam HD-3000**: Another affordable option offering good video quality for remote work or online chats.

Reusing Existing Peripherals to Save Money

1. **Evaluate Your Current Peripherals**: Before purchasing new peripherals, take inventory of what you already have. If your current peripherals are in good working condition, there may be no need to replace

them. For example:

- **Keyboard and Mouse**: If your current keyboard and mouse are in good shape and meet your needs, continue using them. Wired peripherals, in particular, often have a long lifespan.
- **Monitor**: If you already have a functioning monitor, you can save a significant amount by reusing it. Just make sure to check its resolution and available ports to ensure compatibility with your new setup.
- **Headset or Speakers**: These peripherals often have a long lifespan and can be reused as long as they provide satisfactory sound quality.

2. **Adapting Peripherals**:

- **Adapters and Converters**: If you have older peripherals, like a monitor with a VGA port, you can use adapters to connect them to modern ports (HDMI, DisplayPort) on your new PC. This allows you to reuse your older equipment without compromising quality.

3. **Prioritizing Purchases**:

- If you need to buy new peripherals, prioritize those that will have the most impact on your experience. For instance, a good monitor or an ergonomic mouse can significantly enhance your comfort and productivity, while you can wait to replace other less critical accessories.

Conclusion

It's entirely possible to find high-performing peripherals at affordable prices by choosing the right brands and models. Additionally, by reusing existing peripherals, you can save even more without compromising the quality of your user experience. The goal is to maximize comfort and productivity while staying within your budget.

Preparation: Tools and Workspace

Before you start assembling your PC, it's essential to prepare your workspace and gather all necessary tools. An organized workspace and a few simple safety precautions will ensure that the assembly process goes smoothly. Here's how to prepare.

List of Necessary Tools

To assemble a PC, you don't need a lot of tools, but the following items are essential:

1. **Phillips Head Screwdriver**: The main tool you'll need is a medium-sized Phillips head screwdriver (typically size #2). This will be used to screw in the motherboard, case, and other components.

2. **Antistatic Wrist Strap (Optional but Recommended)**: An antistatic wrist strap helps prevent damage to sensitive components due to static electricity. If you don't have one, be sure to discharge any static electricity by touching a bare metal

surface (like the unpainted part of your power supply) before handling components.

3. **Tweezers or Small Needle-Nose Pliers**: A small pair of tweezers or needle-nose pliers can be useful for handling screws or small connectors in tight spaces.

4. **Thermal Paste (if needed)**: If you're using a CPU cooler that doesn't come with pre-applied thermal paste, you'll need to apply a thin layer of thermal paste on the processor. Make sure to use quality thermal paste.

5. **Cable Ties (Zip Ties or Velcro Straps)**: These are useful for organizing cables inside the case, which improves airflow and makes future maintenance easier.

6. **USB Installation Drive**: If you plan to install the operating system via a USB stick, prepare it in advance with the ISO of your OS (Windows, Linux, etc.).

Preparing a Clean and Safe Workspace

1. Choosing an Adequate Workspace:

- **Flat, Stable Surface**: Set up on a flat and stable surface, like a desk or table.

Make sure you have enough space to lay out all the components and tools without stacking them.

- **Sufficient Lighting**: Good lighting is essential to clearly see what you're doing, especially when working with small connectors and screws.
- **Non-Conductive Surface**: Preferably work on a non-conductive surface (like wood or plastic) to reduce the risk of static electricity.

2. **Organizing the Components**:

- **Unpack the Components**: Carefully remove all components from their packaging and lay them out on the table. Keep screws, cables, and other accessories organized for easy access.
- **Identify the Parts**: Take time to identify each component (CPU, motherboard, RAM, GPU, etc.) and read the manuals to understand their respective installation steps.

3. **Preparing a Screw Management System**:

- **Use a Small Bowl or Box**: Use a small bowl or box to store screws while assembling your PC. This prevents them from getting lost during the process.

Safety Considerations (Static Electricity, Precautions)

1. **Managing Static Electricity**:
   - **Use an Antistatic Wrist Strap**: Wear an antistatic wrist strap attached to a grounded metal surface to avoid electrostatic discharge (ESD) that could damage your components.
   - **Discharge Static**: If you don't have an antistatic wrist strap, touch a metal part of your case or power supply regularly to discharge any static electricity from your body.

By following these steps and using the right tools, you'll be well-prepared to assemble your PC in a safe and organized manner, reducing the risk of damage to components and ensuring a smoother build process.

- **Safety Considerations (Static Electricity, Precautions)**

1. **Discharge Static Electricity**:
   - **Touch the Metal Case**: If you don't have an antistatic wrist strap, regularly touch an unpainted metal part of your PC case (like the frame of the power supply) to discharge any static electricity before handling internal components.

2. **Handle Components with Care**:

- **Hold Components by the Edges**: Avoid touching the circuit boards or connectors directly. Hold motherboards, GPUs, and other components by their edges to minimize the risk of damage.
- **Avoid Static-Prone Environments**: Don't work on carpeted surfaces, and wear clothing that doesn't generate static (like cotton instead of wool or polyester).

3. **Work Slowly and Carefully**:

- Take your time with each step. Working slowly reduces the risk of mistakes and damage to components.

4. **Don't Force Anything**:

- If something doesn't fit easily, don't force it. Check the instructions and make sure parts are properly aligned.

By following these tips, you ensure that your workspace is well-organized and safe, making the assembly of your PC easier and more enjoyable. Good preparation is key to completing your project stress-free and without risking damage to your components.

Step 1: Preparing the Case

Now that your workspace is ready and you have all the necessary tools, it's time to start the assembly process by preparing the case. This first step involves getting the case ready to receive the components, which includes installing the standoffs for the motherboard and managing any pre-installed cables. Here's how to proceed:

1. **Unbox and Inspect the Case**:

   - Carefully unbox your case and inspect it for any shipping damage.
   - Remove both side panels to give yourself easy access to the inside of the case.

2. **Install the Motherboard Standoffs**:

   - Identify the locations where the motherboard will be mounted inside the case. Most cases come with standoffs (small metal or plastic posts) pre-installed, but if not, you'll need to install them yourself.
   - The standoffs prevent the motherboard from touching the case directly, avoiding short circuits. Screw them into the pre-drilled holes

that correspond to your motherboard's form factor (ATX, Micro-ATX, etc.).

3. **Organize Cables and Check for Pre-Installed Fans**:

- Take note of any pre-installed fans and their connections. You may need to connect these to the motherboard or a fan controller later.
- Begin organizing the case's cables, such as the front panel connectors (power button, reset button, USB ports, audio jacks), by routing them through the appropriate cable management channels or openings.

4. **Prepare for Power Supply Installation (if not already installed)**:

- If your case doesn't have the power supply pre-installed, identify the location for the PSU (usually at the bottom or top rear of the case).
- Slide the power supply into place, aligning it with the mounting holes, and secure it with screws.

Taking these steps ensures that your case is properly set up to accommodate the installation of the motherboard and other components in the following steps. This preparation is crucial for a smooth and successful PC building experience.

Step 1: Preparing the Case

The first step in assembling your PC is to prepare the case, which will house all the components. This involves unboxing the case, installing the standoffs for the motherboard, and setting up cable management. Here's how to proceed:

Unboxing and Preparing the Case

1. **Unboxing the Case**:

    - **Open the Box Carefully**: When you

receive your case, open the box carefully to avoid scratching or damaging the surface of the case. Remove any foam or plastic protective materials and place the case on a flat, stable surface.

- **Remove the Side Panels**: Most cases have side panels secured with thumb screws or Phillips screws. Remove these screws and take off the panels to access the interior of the case. This gives you space to work and install components.
- **Check the Contents**: Inside the case, you'll typically find a small bag containing screws, standoffs, and other accessories. Make sure you have everything you need before you start the assembly.

2. **Inspecting the Case**:

- **Check Preinstalled Connectors and Cables**: Some cases come with preinstalled cables for USB ports, the power button, LED indicators, and more. Identify these cables so you can connect them correctly to the motherboard later.

- **Ensure Dust Filters Are in Place**: If your case has dust filters, check that they are properly installed. These filters are usually located at the front, bottom, and sometimes on the top of the case.

Installing the Standoffs for the Motherboard

1. **Identify the Mounting Points**:

   - Most cases have pre-drilled holes that correspond to the standard mounting points on a motherboard. These holes are typically labeled for ATX, Micro-ATX, or Mini-ITX motherboards.
   - Before installing the standoffs, identify which holes match your motherboard's form factor.

2. **Install the Standoffs**:

   - **Standoffs** are small metal or plastic posts that raise the motherboard slightly above the case's metal surface to prevent short circuits.
   - Using the screws provided, install the standoffs in the appropriate holes for your motherboard. Most ATX motherboards will require around nine

standoffs.

3. **Double-Check the Standoff Placement**:

- Ensure that the standoffs align with the screw holes on your motherboard. Each screw hole on the motherboard should line up with a standoff beneath it.

By carefully unboxing, inspecting, and preparing your case, you set the stage for a smooth assembly process. Installing the standoffs correctly is crucial as it ensures your motherboard is securely mounted and isolated from the metal chassis, preventing potential electrical issues.

Installing the Standoffs for the Motherboard

Standoffs are small metal supports that attach to the case and on which the motherboard will be screwed. They keep the motherboard elevated, preventing it from touching the case directly, which could cause a short circuit.

1. Locating the Mounting Points:

- **Identify the Mounting Holes**: The motherboard has several mounting holes that correspond to the mounting points in the case. Cases are designed to accommodate different motherboard sizes (ATX, Micro-ATX, Mini-ITX), and the mounting holes are labeled accordingly.

- **Align the Standoffs**: Align the standoffs with the mounting holes that match your motherboard's form factor. Only install standoffs in the holes that correspond to your specific motherboard model.

2. Screwing in the Standoffs:

- **Install the Standoffs**: Use the standoffs provided with the case. Screw them into the designated holes in the case using your Phillips screwdriver. Ensure that each standoff is securely in place and aligned with a mounting hole on the motherboard.
- **Check Stability**: After installing the standoffs, make sure they are firmly attached and stable. There should be no standoff in a hole that doesn't correspond to a motherboard mounting hole, as this could cause issues during installation.

By carefully installing the standoffs, you ensure that your motherboard will be properly supported and isolated from the metal chassis, preventing any potential short circuits and ensuring a smooth and secure assembly process.

Cable Management

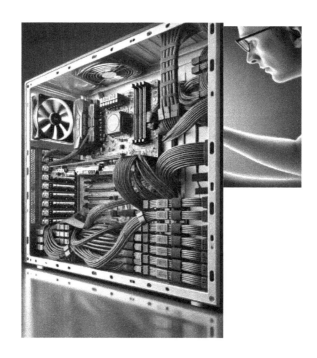

Good cable management is essential for ensuring optimal airflow within the case and keeping the interior clean and organized. It

also makes future upgrades or repairs easier.

1. **Plan Cable Routing**:

   - **Identify Cable Pass-Throughs**: Most modern cases are equipped with holes or channels specifically designed to route cables behind the motherboard. Identify these pass-throughs and plan how you will route the power cables, hard drive cables, and fan cables.
   - **Position Unused Cables**: If your power supply has cables you won't be using, such as extra connectors, neatly store them behind the motherboard or in a cable management compartment to prevent them from obstructing airflow.

2. **Cable Ties**:

- **Using Cable Ties**: To keep the cables in place, use cable ties (zip ties) or Velcro straps. Group the cables together in small bundles and secure them to the designated attachment points within the case. This prevents them from moving around during transport or use, and improves airflow inside the case.

Check Airflow: Once the cables are secured, ensure they do not obstruct the airflow from the fans. The cables should not block the front, rear, or graphics card fans.

By following these steps, you effectively and neatly prepare your case, making it easier to install components and ensuring good ventilation for your system. A well-prepared case is the foundation of a functional and reliable PC.

Step 2: Installing the Processor and RAM on the Motherboard

This step involves installing the processor (CPU) and memory (RAM) onto the motherboard. It's a delicate process, as the CPU is one of the most sensitive components of your PC. However, by carefully following the instructions, you can do it without difficulty. Here's how to proceed.

Installing the Processor (CPU)

- **Illustration: How to Install the Processor**

Opening the CPU Socket:

- **Locate the CPU Socket**: Find the CPU

socket on the motherboard. It's a square area with a metal cover (for Intel processors) or a lever (for AMD processors).

- **For Intel Processors**: Gently push down on the metal lever beside the socket and lift it to open the cover.
- **For AMD Processors**: Lift the lever beside the socket to open the bracket.

Aligning the Processor:

- Carefully remove the processor from its packaging by holding it by the edges, avoiding contact with the pins or the gold contacts underneath.
- Align the processor with the socket by matching the corner marked with a small gold triangle on both the processor and the socket. This triangle indicates the correct orientation for insertion.
- Gently place the processor into the socket without applying force. It should naturally fit into place.

Securing the Processor:

- **For Intel Processors**: Lower the metal cover over the processor and then lower the lever to lock it in place.

- **For AMD Processors**: Simply lower the lever to secure the processor.

Applying Thermal Paste

- **If your CPU cooler (fan or liquid cooling system) does not have pre-applied thermal paste, you'll need to apply a small amount.**
  - The CPU cooler is then directly mounted onto the CPU after the thermal paste application. This ensures optimal contact between the cooler's heatsink and the CPU, allowing efficient dissipation of the heat generated by the processor.

Applying Thermal Paste

Amount of Paste:

- Apply a small amount of thermal paste (about the size of a small pea or a grain of rice) to the center of the processor. The thermal paste helps to transfer heat from the CPU to the heatsink of the cooler.

- **Spreading the Paste (Optional):**

- It is not necessary to spread the paste, as tightening the cooler will evenly distribute the paste. However, if you prefer, you can use a plastic spatula or a piece of cardboard to spread the paste into a thin, even layer.

Install the RAM in the Correct Slots

1.1. Identify the RAM Slots:

- **RAM Slots**: The motherboard typically has two or four slots for RAM. These slots are often color-coded in pairs to indicate dual channels.
- Refer to your motherboard's manual to determine which slots to use for a dual-channel configuration (usually, slots 1 and 3 or 2 and 4 are used together).

2. Installing the RAM:

- **Align the RAM**:

- Remove the RAM modules from their packaging and locate the notch on the bottom edge. This notch must align with the small ridge in the motherboard slot.
- Carefully align the RAM with the slot, ensuring the notch lines up correctly.

- **Insert the RAM**:

  - Once aligned, firmly insert the RAM into the slot by pressing evenly on both ends until you hear a click. This click indicates that the clips on either side of the slot have locked the RAM into place.
  - If you have more than two RAM modules, install them in the recommended slots to enable dual-channel mode, which will improve performance.

By following these steps, you will have correctly installed the processor and RAM on your motherboard. This prepares the motherboard to be mounted in the case and to receive other components. It is crucial to work carefully during this step, as the CPU and RAM are delicate but essential components for your PC's proper operation.

Step 3: Mounting the Motherboard in the Case

Once the processor and RAM are installed on the motherboard, the next step is to mount the motherboard in the case. This step involves positioning the motherboard correctly, securing it using the standoffs installed earlier, and connecting the basic cables, including those for power and fans. Here's how to proceed.

Position the Motherboard and Screw in the Standoffs

1. Illustration: Positioning the Motherboard

- **Align the Motherboard**:

112

- Carefully place the motherboard into the case, aligning the mounting holes on the motherboard with the standoffs you installed in the case in the previous step.
- Ensure that the I/O ports (USB, Ethernet, audio, etc.) on the back of the motherboard align correctly with the I/O shield at the rear of the case. This shield may be pre-installed or come with the motherboard and should be installed before the motherboard.

- **Check the Alignment of the Connectors**:
  - Before screwing in, verify that the motherboard is properly seated, with the connectors aligned with the cutouts in the case. If necessary, adjust the position slightly for a perfect fit.

2. Screw in the Motherboard

- **Secure the Motherboard**:
  - Use the screws provided with the case to secure the motherboard to the standoffs. Screw in the motherboard

so that it is securely held in place, but avoid over-tightening to prevent damaging the board.

- Start by screwing in the opposite corners of the motherboard to ensure proper alignment, then proceed to screw in the remaining holes. Typically, there are 6 to 9 screws to secure, depending on the size of the motherboard.

- **Check the Stability**:

  - Once the motherboard is secured, check that it is stable and there is no movement. If it shifts, recheck the screws and adjust them as needed.

Connect the Basic Cables (Power, Fans)

1.1. Connecting the Power Supply (PSU) to the Motherboard

Main Power Cable (24-Pin ATX):

- **Locate the main power cable** from the power supply (a large 24-pin connector) and plug it into the corresponding 24-pin connector on the motherboard. This cable provides the primary power to the motherboard.

Finding the 24-Pin ATX Power Connector on the Motherboard:

1. **Location**: The 24-pin connector is typically located on the right side of the motherboard, near the edge. It is often situated to the right of the RAM slots, either at the top or middle of the motherboard. It is easily recognizable by its large size.

2. **Connector**: The 24-pin connector is the largest connector on the motherboard. It primarily powers the motherboard, enabling all its components to function.

3. **Orientation**: When connecting, the cable must be aligned correctly with the connector. There is a latch on the connector that clicks into place to secure the cable.

When looking at a motherboard, the 24-pin connector is often the most visible and most important for the main power supply.

- Ensure that the connector is fully inserted until you hear a click.

CPU Power Cable (8-Pin or 4-Pin ATX12V):

Next, locate the CPU power cable, which is often an 8-pin connector (sometimes split into two 4-pin connectors). It typically connects near the CPU socket, at the top of the motherboard.

- **Carefully plug it into the corresponding connector. This cable specifically powers the processor.**

2. Connecting the Fan Cables

- **Case Fans:**

The case fans usually connect to specific headers on the motherboard, labeled "CHA_FAN" or "SYS_FAN." These headers are dedicated to connecting case fans.

- **CHA_FAN (Chassis Fan)**: This header is specifically designed for case fans that help maintain airflow inside the case. It allows the motherboard to control the fan speed based on the detected temperature, ensuring optimal cooling.

- **SYS_FAN (System Fan)**: This is another header for system fans. Like CHA_FAN, it is used to connect case fans. Sometimes, a motherboard may have multiple SYS_FAN headers to manage several case fans.

These headers allow fan control through the BIOS or management software, adjusting fan speeds according to the system's cooling needs.

- **Identify these headers on your motherboard by consulting the manual.**
- **Plug each fan cable into the corresponding header.** This will enable the motherboard to control the fan speeds based on the system temperature.

CPU Fan:

- If you have installed a CPU cooler with a fan, connect it to the "CPU_FAN" header on the motherboard. This connector is usually located near the CPU socket.

- **Ensure that this connector is securely in place,** as it is crucial for the proper functioning and cooling of your processor.

2. Connecting Internal Peripheral Cables (Optional)

- **USB, Audio, and Case Button Cables**:
- The cables for the front USB ports, audio, and power/reset buttons of the case also need to be connected to the motherboard. These cables are usually labeled, and the corresponding headers on the motherboard are identified in the motherboard manual.

- **Plug these cables into the appropriate headers** so that the ports and buttons on your case are functional.

SATA Cables for Hard Drives/SSDs:

- If you have already installed hard drives or SSDs, connect them to the SATA ports on the motherboard using the provided SATA cables. These cables are typically flat and thin, with "L"-shaped connectors. SATA (Serial ATA) cables are used to connect hard drives (HDDs), SSDs, and other internal storage devices to your motherboard. Here are some key points about SATA cables:

1. Shape and Connectors:

SATA Cables:
- **SATA cables are generally flat and thin.**
- They have "L"-shaped connectors on each end, which help ensure they are inserted correctly into the SATA ports.

Function:
- SATA cables transfer data between the hard drive/SSD and the motherboard.
- Another cable, known as the SATA power cable, powers the drive, while the SATA cable handles the data.

SATA Port on the Motherboard:
- The motherboard has multiple SATA ports where SATA cables connect, enabling communication between the drives and the rest of the system.

Usage:

- You plug one end of the SATA cable into the hard drive or SSD and the other end into the SATA port on the motherboard.
- SATA cables are essential for the proper functioning of storage drives in a PC.

By following these steps, you will have successfully installed the motherboard into the case, ensuring that all essential cables are connected. This prepares your system for the next steps, such as installing the graphics card and connecting the hard drives. Once these cables are plugged in, your PC begins to take shape, and you are well advanced in the assembly process.

Step 4: Installing the Cooling System

The cooling system is crucial for keeping your processor and other components at safe temperatures, especially when using your PC for demanding tasks. This step covers the installation of fans or a liquid cooling system, as well as important considerations for airflow to ensure effective cooling.

Illustration: Installing Fans or Liquid Cooling

1. Installing Case Fans:

Positioning the Fans:

- Case fans are typically installed at the front, rear, and sometimes at the top or bottom of the case. The goal is to create optimal airflow through the case.

- Generally, the front fans draw cool air into the case, while the rear and top fans expel hot air.
- Secure the fans by screwing them into the designated spots in the case. Ensure that the arrows on the side of the fans (indicating the direction of airflow) point in the correct direction.

Connecting the Fans:

- Connect the fan cables to the appropriate headers on the motherboard (usually labeled "CHA_FAN" or "SYS_FAN"). You can also use a fan controller or hub if your motherboard doesn't have enough connectors.

2. Installing Liquid Cooling

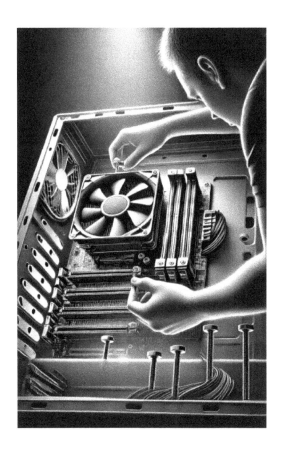

- **Mounting the Radiator**:
- If you're using a liquid cooling system, start by mounting the radiator in the designated spot in the case. This could be at the front,

top, or rear of the case, depending on the case design and the size of the radiator.

- Screw the radiator in place using the provided screws. If the radiator is equipped with fans, ensure that they are mounted to either draw in or expel air as needed.

Mounting the Waterblock on the CPU:

- The waterblock is the part of the liquid cooling system that attaches directly to the processor. Before installing it, make sure that the CPU has thermal paste applied (either pre-applied on the waterblock or added during the CPU installation).

- Position the waterblock on the processor and secure it using the provided brackets or screws. Follow the manufacturer's instructions to ensure a correct and secure mounting.
- Connect the waterblock cables (power and possibly RGB control) to the motherboard or power supply, according to the manufacturer's instructions.

Connecting the Pumps and Fans:

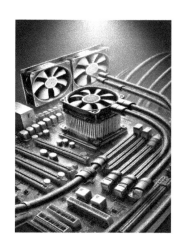

- Liquid cooling systems often include fans mounted on the radiator and an integrated pump. Connect the fans to the fan headers on the motherboard, and the pump to a power connector (usually a "PUMP_FAN" header or directly to the power supply via a SATA connector).

The Cooling Pump:

•

A pump in a liquid cooling system for a PC is an essential component that circulates the coolant through the system to absorb and dissipate heat from the processor (CPU). Here's what it typically looks like:

1. Shape and Structure:

- The pump is often integrated into the waterblock (the part that attaches to the CPU) or attached to the radiator.
- It typically has a cylindrical or rectangular shape, with ports for the coolant's inlet and

outlet.

2. Connectors:

- The pump usually has a power connector, often a 3- or 4-pin connector, or a SATA connector for power.
- It may also have a connector to plug into a "PUMP_FAN" header on the motherboard.

3. Function:

- The pump works to circulate the coolant through the loop, passing through the radiator to cool down before returning to the CPU.
- Pumps are crucial for maintaining a constant flow of coolant, ensuring that the cooling system operates efficiently.

Airflow Considerations

Good airflow is crucial for maintaining stable temperatures and preventing overheating. Here are some tips for optimizing airflow in your case:

1. Fan Orientation:

- **Intake Air**: Place fans at the front and sometimes the bottom of the case to draw cool air from the outside into the case.

- **Exhaust Air**: Fans at the rear and top of the case should expel hot air out of the case. This setup helps create a constant airflow through the case, efficiently removing the heat generated by the components.

2. Airflow Balance:

- **Positive Airflow**: This occurs when you have more fans bringing cool air into the case than fans expelling hot air. This type of airflow can help reduce dust buildup, as the air pressure inside the case is higher than outside.
- **Negative Airflow**: This occurs when you have more fans expelling hot air than bringing in cool air. While this can remove heat more quickly, it may also lead to more dust entering the case.

3. Cable Management:

- Proper cable routing is essential to avoid obstructing airflow. Poorly managed cables can block air passage and reduce cooling efficiency. Use cable ties to keep cables out of the airflow path.

4. Case Cleanliness:

- Dust filters should be cleaned regularly to prevent dust from reducing airflow. A clean case not only improves cooling but also extends the lifespan of your components.

By following these steps to install your cooling system and considering airflow, you ensure that your PC remains at an optimal temperature, even under heavy workloads. Good cooling extends the lifespan of components and ensures stable performance, which is essential for any well-built PC.

Step 5: Installing the GPU and Storage

Installing the graphics card (GPU) and storage devices (hard drives and SSDs) is a key step in completing your PC build. This step involves securing the graphics card into the correct PCIe slot and mounting your storage drives in the designated slots in the case.

Mounting the Graphics Card (GPU)

1. Illustration: Mounting the Graphics Card:

- **Identify the PCIe Slot**:

- **The graphics card is installed in the PCIe x16 slot, which is usually the longest slot on the motherboard and often located near the processor. If you have multiple PCIe x16 slots, use the one closest to the processor for the best performance.**

Preparing the PCIe Slot:

- **Before inserting the graphics card, remove the expansion slot covers at the back of the case that correspond to the GPU's slots.** These covers are secured with screws or clips, which you need to remove to create space for the graphics card's display ports (HDMI, DisplayPort, etc.).

Inserting the Graphics Card:

- **Hold the graphics card by the edges, align it with the PCIe x16 slot, and press it firmly downward until you hear a click.** This click indicates that the card is securely inserted and that the PCIe slot's retention clip is engaged.
- **Ensure that the card is parallel to the motherboard and that the connectors are properly seated.**

Securing the Graphics Card:

- **Once the card is in place, use the screws you previously removed to secure the metal bracket of the graphics card to the back of the case.** This ensures the card is stable and prevents any movement during transport or use.

2. Connecting Power to the GPU:

Plugging in the Power Cables:

- **Most modern graphics cards require additional power.** Connect the PCIe power cables from your power supply to the graphics card (6-pin, 8-pin, or a combination of both, depending on the model).
- **Make sure these cables are securely connected to prevent accidental disconnection.**

Installing Hard Drives (HDD) and SSDs:

1. Installing Hard Drives (HDD)

Identify the Hard Drive Bays:

- Most cases have specific bays for 3.5-inch hard drives. These bays can be oriented horizontally or vertically, and some come with removable trays or cages to make installation easier.

Mount the Hard Drive:

- Insert the hard drive into an empty bay. If your case uses rails or trays, secure the hard drive with the provided screws or use the tool-less mechanism if available.
- For bays without rails, directly screw the

hard drive into place using four screws (two on each side) to secure it.

Connect the Cables:

- Connect a SATA cable between the hard drive and an available SATA port on the motherboard. Then, plug a SATA power cable from the power supply into the hard drive. These cables are flat and have an "L" shape to ensure correct connection.

2. Installing SSDs (SATA and M.2)

SATA SSD (2.5-inch):

- For a 2.5-inch SATA SSD, find an appropriate location in the case, usually next to the hard drive bays or sometimes on the backside of the motherboard tray.
- Secure the SSD using the provided screws or the built-in mounts in the case.
- Connect the SSD to the motherboard using a SATA cable and plug in a SATA power cable.

M.2 SSD:

- M.2 SSDs mount directly onto the motherboard in an M.2 slot. Locate the M.2 slot on the motherboard, typically near the

CPU or PCIe slots.

- Insert the M.2 SSD into the slot at a 30-degree angle, then gently press it down until it lies flat against the motherboard.
- Secure the SSD with the small screw provided with the motherboard or the SSD. This screw is placed at the end of the SSD to hold it in place.

3. Checking the Connections

Double-Check:

- Ensure that all cables (SATA, power) are properly connected and securely fastened.
- Also, make sure that the drives are securely mounted in their respective slots to prevent any movement or vibration.

By following these steps, you will have successfully installed the graphics card and storage devices in your PC. These components are crucial for graphical performance and storage capacity, and proper installation ensures that your PC will function optimally. You are now ready to move on to configuring and testing your system.

Step 6: Connecting the Power Supply (PSU)

The Power Supply Unit (PSU) is the component

of the computer that provides power to all the other components.

What is a PSU?

The PSU (Power Supply Unit) converts the alternating current (AC) from your wall outlet into direct current (DC) that your PC components can use. It then distributes this power to various components through multiple cables.

Main PSU Connections:

1. Main Power Cable (24-Pin ATX):

- This cable powers the motherboard and must be connected to the 24-pin connector on the motherboard.
- It's the largest cable and is essential for providing power to the motherboard, allowing the computer to start.

2. CPU Power Cable (4-Pin or 8-Pin ATX12V):

- Directly powers the processor (CPU).
- This cable is usually located near the processor on the motherboard.

3. PCIe Cables:

- These cables power energy-intensive components like graphics cards (GPUs).
- They connect directly to graphics cards via 6-pin or 8-pin connectors.

4. SATA Cables:

- These cables power hard drives (HDDs), SSDs, and sometimes additional peripherals like optical drives.
- SATA cables are thin with "L"-shaped connectors.

5. Molex Cables:

- Although less commonly used today, Molex cables can power some older peripherals or fans.

PSU Connection Process:

- **1. Installing the PSU in the**

Case:

- The PSU is typically placed either at the bottom or the top of the case, depending on the design.
- Secure it with screws to ensure it is firmly attached.

2. Connecting the Cables:

- **Connect the 24-pin cable** to the motherboard first.
- Next, **connect the CPU power cable** (8-pin or 4-pin).
- **Plug in the PCIe cables** to the graphics cards if necessary.
- **Connect the SATA cables** to the hard drives and SSDs.
- Organize and tie down the cables to avoid clutter and improve airflow.

Importance of Proper PSU Connection:

- A proper PSU connection ensures that all components receive stable and adequate power, which is crucial for the system's proper functioning and longevity.

Connecting the PSU to all the components of

your PC is a critical step. It ensures that each component receives the necessary power to operate correctly. Here's how to connect all the power supply connectors and check cable management for optimal airflow and a tidy interior.

Illustration: Plugging in All PSU Connectors:

- **1. Connecting the Main Connectors**

Main Power Cable (24-Pin ATX):

- This is the largest and widest cable. It connects to the 24-pin connector on the motherboard, usually located on the right side of the motherboard.
- Align the connector with the port, then press firmly until it clicks into place, ensuring a secure connection.

CPU Power Cable (8-Pin or 4-Pin ATX12V):

- This cable, typically located at the top of the motherboard, is essential for powering the processor. It can be either an 8-pin or 4-pin connector, depending on the motherboard.
- Plug this cable into the corresponding connector near the CPU socket. As with the 24-pin connector, make sure it is fully engaged.

2. Connecting the PCIe Cables for the GPU

PCIe Power Cables:

- If your graphics card requires additional power, you will need to connect one or more PCIe cables (6-pin or 8-pin) from the PSU to the graphics card.
- Insert these cables into the corresponding PCIe ports on the graphics card, ensuring adequate power for the GPU, especially for demanding graphical tasks.

3. Connecting the Cables for Storage (HDD and SSD)

SATA Power Cables:

- Hard drives (HDD) and SSDs require power via SATA cables. Each SATA cable connects directly from the power supply to the power connectors on each drive.
- Insert the SATA connector into the power port on the drive until it is securely in place. Make sure all hard drives and SSDs are properly connected to avoid data loss or device failure.

4. Connecting Other Components

Fans and Other Peripherals:

- Some fans or peripherals may require direct power from the PSU via Molex or SATA connectors. Check each component to ensure it receives the appropriate power.
- Connect these cables to the appropriate headers or connectors on the motherboard or directly to the PSU.

Cable Management Check

1. Organizing Cables for Optimal Airflow

Cable Routing:

- Route cables behind the motherboard tray or through designated cable management channels in the case. This clears space around the motherboard and other components, facilitating airflow.
- Avoid leaving cables hanging or obstructing fans, as this could impede cooling and reduce system efficiency.

Cable Ties:

- Use cable ties or Velcro straps to group cables neatly. Attach them to anchor points in the case to keep them in place.
- Good cable management not only improves the internal aesthetics of your PC but also its performance by reducing airflow obstructions.

2. Final Connection Check

Double-Check:

- Before closing the case, review all connections to ensure no cable is missed or improperly connected. Verify each connection, especially the main power, CPU, GPU, and SATA cables.
- Also, make sure all cables are securely fastened and that

there is no excessive tension or sharp bends that could damage the cables over time.

Preliminary Test:

- Once all cables are connected and organized, plug your PC into a power outlet, but do not start it yet. Press the power button to check that the fans start spinning and the LEDs light up, indicating that the system is receiving power correctly.

By following these steps, you will have properly connected the power supply to all components of your PC and managed the cables efficiently. Good cable management and secure connections ensure not only a functional and high-performing PC but also a clean and easy-to-maintain interior. You are now ready to proceed to the final setup and operating system installation.

Step 7: Verifying and Starting the PC

This step is crucial to ensure that everything is correctly connected and that your PC is ready to function. Before proceeding to the first boot, a final check of the connections is essential. Then, you can start your PC and access the BIOS to configure the basic settings.

Checking the Connections

1. Double-Check Internal Connections

Power:

- Ensure that all power cables are correctly connected: the 24-pin main cable to the motherboard, the CPU power cable (8-pin or 4-pin), the PCIe cables to the GPU, and the SATA cables to the hard drives and SSDs.
- Verify that all connectors are fully engaged and that no cable is loose.

Data Cables:

- Check the SATA cables between the storage drives (HDD/SSD) and the motherboard. Ensure they are well-connected and not excessively bent.

Fans and Cooling:

- Ensure all fans are connected to the motherboard headers or a fan hub and are securely mounted.
- Check that the CPU cooling system (fan or water block) is correctly connected and secured.

2. Check External Connections

Monitor:

- Connect your monitor to the graphics card via an HDMI, DisplayPort, or DVI cable. Ensure the monitor is powered on and set to the correct video input.

Keyboard and Mouse:

- Plug your keyboard and mouse into USB ports on the motherboard or case.

Power:

- Plug the PSU's main power cable into a wall outlet. Make sure the PSU switch is in the "On" (I) position.

First Boot and Accessing the BIOS

1. First Boot

Press the Power Button:

Starting Your PC and Accessing the BIOS

1. Power On the PC

- **Press the Power Button:** Located at the front of your case, press the power button to turn on your PC. If everything is connected correctly, you should see the fans start spinning, LEDs light up, and the monitor display the motherboard manufacturer's logo or a startup screen.

- **Listen for Beeps:** Pay attention to the motherboard's beep codes. A single short beep typically indicates that everything is functioning properly. Multiple beeps or no video signal may suggest a connection issue or a problem with a component.

2. Accessing the BIOS

- **Enter the BIOS:** As soon as you power on your PC, press the key indicated to enter the BIOS setup (usually "Delete," "F2," or "Esc," depending on the motherboard). This information is generally briefly displayed on the screen during the startup process.

Following these steps will ensure that your PC is correctly assembled and powered on. Entering the BIOS allows you to configure essential system settings and verify that all components are recognized and functioning properly.

-

- **Troubleshooting BIOS Access and Component Verification**

1. Troubleshooting BIOS Access

- **Retry Entering BIOS:** If you are unable to enter the BIOS, restart your PC and try pressing the BIOS entry key repeatedly. This can help if the timing was off during your initial attempt. Ensure you press the key immediately after powering on the PC to increase your chances of success.

2. Checking Basic Settings in the BIOS

For those unfamiliar with computer hardware, entering the BIOS and verifying components might seem daunting. However, with a step-by-step approach, it becomes manageable. Here's a guide to help you navigate the BIOS and check your components:

Step 1: Entering the BIOS

- **How to Enter:** As soon as you press the power button to turn on your PC, begin pressing the key designated for accessing the BIOS. Common keys include "Delete," "F2," or "Esc." You should see a black screen with startup indications, and it is here that you need to press the designated key to enter the BIOS.

Step 2: Verifying Components

- **Navigate the BIOS Menu:** Once inside the BIOS, you will be greeted with a configuration screen. The layout can vary based on your motherboard's manufacturer, but the basic options are generally similar.

  - **Check the CPU:** Locate the section of the BIOS that displays information about the CPU. This area will confirm if the processor is correctly detected by the system.

- **Verify Memory (RAM):** Find the memory or RAM section to ensure that all installed memory modules are recognized and operating correctly.

- **Inspect Storage Devices:** Navigate to the storage or SATA configuration section to confirm that all connected storage devices (HDDs and SSDs) are detected.

- **Review GPU Detection:** If applicable, check the GPU section or the system summary to ensure that the graphics card is recognized.

- **Confirm Device Settings:** Ensure that your storage devices are configured correctly (e.g., set to the proper AHCI mode if necessary). Check the boot order to confirm that your system is set to boot from the appropriate drive.

3. Additional BIOS Adjustments

- **Adjust Boot Order:** Set the primary boot device to your intended operating system drive, which ensures that the PC will boot from the correct drive.

- **Save and Exit:** After verifying that all components are detected and configured correctly, navigate to the "Save & Exit" option in the BIOS menu. Confirm your choices and allow the PC to reboot.

By following these steps, you will ensure that all components are recognized and properly configured, setting the stage for a successful operating system installation and overall system functionality.

Guide de Dépannage pour le BIOS et Vérification des Composants

1. Vérification des Composants dans le BIOS

Processeur :

- **Où chercher :** Accédez à l'écran d'accueil du BIOS ou à un onglet appelé "Main" ou "System Information". Cette section affiche les informations du processeur installé.
- **Que vérifier :** Assurez-vous que le modèle du processeur affiché correspond au processeur que vous avez installé. Par exemple, si vous avez installé un "Intel Core i7" ou un "AMD Ryzen 5", cela doit être indiqué correctement dans le BIOS.

RAM :

- **Où chercher :** Toujours dans l'onglet "Main" ou "System Information", vérifiez la quantité totale de RAM installée.
- **Que vérifier :** Confirmez que la quantité de RAM affichée correspond à ce que vous avez installé (par exemple, si vous avez installé 16 Go de RAM, le BIOS doit afficher "16 GB"). De plus, vérifiez la vitesse de la RAM affichée (par exemple, "3200 MHz") pour s'assurer qu'elle

correspond à la vitesse spécifiée par le fabricant.

Stockage (Disques durs et SSD) :

- **Où chercher :** Recherchez un onglet ou une section appelée "Storage", "Boot", ou "SATA Configuration".
- **Que vérifier :** Vérifiez que tous les disques durs et SSD que vous avez installés sont détectés. Par exemple, un SSD de 500 Go et un disque dur de 1 To devraient apparaître dans cette section.

2. Configurer l'Ordre de Démarrage (Boot Order)

Accéder aux Paramètres de Boot :

- **Où chercher :** Recherchez un onglet ou une section appelée "Boot" ou "Boot Order".
- **Que faire :** Vous verrez une liste des périphériques de stockage, tels que SSD, disques durs, clés USB, etc. Le périphérique en haut de la liste est celui que le PC essaiera de démarrer en premier.

Configurer l'Ordre de Démarrage :

- **Comment faire :** Utilisez les touches

fléchées pour sélectionner le disque sur lequel vous installerez votre système d'exploitation (généralement un SSD). Ensuite, utilisez une touche indiquée à l'écran (souvent "+" ou "-") pour déplacer ce disque en haut de la liste.

Enregistrer les Modifications et Quitter :

- **Comment faire :** Après avoir configuré l'ordre de démarrage, recherchez l'option "Save & Exit" ou "Save Changes and Exit" (souvent située dans un onglet en haut de l'écran). Sélectionnez cette option pour enregistrer vos paramètres et redémarrer l'ordinateur.

3. Problèmes Potentiels et Solutions

Pas d'Affichage ou Bips d'Alerte :

- **Solution :** Si le PC ne démarre pas correctement ou si vous entendez des bips d'alerte, éteignez-le et vérifiez toutes les connexions. Assurez-vous que la carte graphique est bien insérée dans le slot PCIe, que la RAM est correctement installée et que le processeur est correctement alimenté.

Réinitialisation du BIOS :

- **Solution :** Si le PC ne démarre toujours pas, essayez de réinitialiser le BIOS en utilisant le cavalier de réinitialisation CMOS ou en retirant la pile CMOS pendant quelques minutes avant de la remettre en place. La réinitialisation du BIOS remet les paramètres à leurs valeurs par défaut et peut résoudre les problèmes liés aux paramètres incorrects.

Qu'est-ce que le CMOS ?

CMOS (Complementary Metal-Oxide-Semiconductor) :

- **Définition :** Le CMOS est une technologie utilisée pour les circuits intégrés qui stockent les paramètres du BIOS de l'ordinateur. La pile CMOS alimente une petite mémoire non volatile qui conserve les paramètres du BIOS même lorsque le PC est éteint.

- **Utilisation :** La réinitialisation du CMOS permet de rétablir les paramètres du BIOS à leurs valeurs par défaut, ce qui est utile si des paramètres incorrects empêchent le démarrage du système ou causent d'autres problèmes.

En suivant ces étapes et conseils, vous devriez être en mesure de résoudre les problèmes courants rencontrés lors du démarrage de votre PC et d'assurer une configuration correcte pour l'installation de votre système d'exploitation. Vous êtes maintenant prêt à procéder à la configuration finale et à l'installation du système d'exploitation pour compléter le processus de montage de votre PC.

- **CMOS (Complementary Metal-Oxide-Semiconductor):**

CMOS is a small memory on the motherboard

that stores BIOS settings, such as clock configurations, boot order, and other system settings. It maintains this information even when the PC is powered off.

CMOS Battery:

The CMOS memory is powered by a small battery, often a coin-cell battery, to keep these settings preserved even when the computer is turned off.

What is a CMOS Reset Jumper?

A CMOS reset jumper is a small, three-pin connector on the motherboard used to clear or reset the CMOS memory. By moving the jumper to the reset position, you can restore the BIOS settings to their factory defaults. This can be helpful for troubleshooting issues related to incorrect BIOS settings or if the system fails to start correctly.

4o mini

- **CMOS Jumper:**

A CMOS jumper is a small plastic connector that bridges two metal pins on the motherboard. These pins are connected to the CMOS memory.

CMOS Reset:

By moving the jumper to connect a different pair of pins, you clear the settings stored in the CMOS memory, resetting the BIOS to its default configuration.

How to Reset the BIOS Using the CMOS Jumper:

1. **Power Off Your Computer:** Ensure the PC is completely turned off and unplugged from the power source.

2. **Open the Case:** Remove the side panels of the case to access the motherboard.

3. **Locate the CMOS Jumper:** Find a small block of pins on the motherboard with a plastic jumper on top. It is often located near the CMOS battery and may be labeled "CLR_CMOS," "RESET," or something similar.

4. **Move the Jumper:**

   - **Current Position:** The jumper is usually in the "Run" position, connecting two of the three pins.
   - **Reset Position:** To reset the BIOS, remove the jumper from its current position and place it on the two adjacent pins for a few seconds.
   - **Replace the Jumper:** Return the jumper to its original position.

5. **Power On:** Replace the side panel of the case, plug the power back in, and turn on

the computer. The BIOS should now be reset to its default settings.

Why Use the CMOS Reset Jumper?

- **Troubleshoot Startup Issues:** If your PC fails to start after changing BIOS settings, resetting can resolve the issue.
- **Clear Incorrect Configurations:** If you accidentally configured something in the BIOS that is causing problems, resetting allows you to return to default settings.

Resetting the BIOS will erase all custom settings, so you will need to reconfigure your BIOS after performing this procedure.

In Other Words...:

When your PC doesn't start correctly or if changes in the BIOS are causing issues, it can be useful to reset the BIOS to return to default settings.

What is BIOS and CMOS?

- **BIOS:** This is a program that runs automatically when you power on your computer. It controls the initial steps of the PC startup and ensures that all hardware components are functioning correctly.

- **CMOS:** This is a small memory chip on the motherboard (the main circuit board of your computer) that stores BIOS settings, such as the computer's clock and the boot order of the various drives.

What is a CMOS Jumper?

A CMOS jumper is used to clear or reset the CMOS memory. By temporarily moving the jumper to a different position, you can restore the BIOS settings to their factory defaults.

- **CMOS Jumper:**

A CMOS jumper is a small plastic connector that bridges two metal pins on the motherboard. It is used to connect these pins to perform specific actions, such as resetting the BIOS.

Resetting the CMOS:

This means clearing the BIOS settings and restoring them to their default state, which is the configuration the computer had when it was first purchased.

How to Reset the BIOS Using the CMOS Jumper:

1. **Turn Off the Computer:** Ensure the computer is completely turned off and unplugged from the power source.

2. **Open the Case:** Remove the side panels from the computer case to access the motherboard (the large printed circuit board inside).

3. **Locate the CMOS Jumper:** Look on the motherboard for a small block of pins (typically three) with a small plastic cap on top. This cap is the CMOS jumper.

4. **Move the Jumper:**

   - **Current Position:** The jumper is usually positioned on two of the three pins.
   - **Reset Position:** Remove the jumper from its current position and place it on the other two pins for a few seconds.
   - **Return the Jumper:** Put the jumper back to its original position.

5. **Power On:** Replace the side panel, plug the computer back in, and turn it on. The BIOS

should now be reset, and the computer should start normally.

Why Perform This?

If your computer fails to start or if you have changed settings that cause problems, this method can reset everything to default, often resolving startup issues. After resetting the BIOS, you may need to adjust some settings again to match your configuration (such as the boot order of drives).

By following these steps, you will be able to start your PC for the first time, access the BIOS, and verify that all components are correctly installed and functioning. It's an exciting moment, as it's the first time you'll see your work come to life! Once this step is completed, you're ready to install the operating system and enjoy your new machine.

12. Installing the Operating System

The installation of the operating system (OS) is the final major step before you can fully use your new PC. The OS is the primary software that manages your computer's hardware and software. Here's how to choose the right OS, create a bootable USB drive, install the OS, and finally, install the necessary drivers for everything to work correctly.

Choosing the Operating System (Windows, Linux)

1. Windows:

Why Choose Windows? Windows is the most popular operating system, compatible with most software and games. It is user-friendly for beginners and has extensive support from both hardware manufacturers and software developers.

Available Versions: The most commonly used version is Windows 10, but Windows 11 is also available and offers more modern features. Choose the version that best suits your needs.

2. Linux:

Why Choose Linux? Linux is an open-source, free, and highly flexible operating system. It is especially favored by developers, experienced users, and for servers. Linux is also less demanding on hardware resources and is more secure by default.

Available Distributions: There are many Linux distributions, such as Ubuntu, Fedora, and Linux Mint, each suited to different types of users. Ubuntu is one of the most popular for beginners, as it is easy to install and use.

Creating a Bootable USB Drive

1. Download the OS ISO:

Windows: Go to Microsoft's official website and download the Media Creation Tool for Windows 10 or Windows 11. This tool will allow you to download the Windows ISO image and create a bootable USB drive directly.

Linux: For Linux, download the ISO image of your chosen distribution from the official website (e.g., ubuntu.com for Ubuntu).

What is an ISO Image? An ISO image is a single file that contains an exact copy of everything on a CD, DVD, or Blu-ray. It's like taking a digital photograph of all the content on a disc and putting it into one file. This ISO file can then be used in various ways.

Uses of an ISO Image:

- **Installing Software or Operating Systems:** ISO images are often used to distribute operating systems (like Windows or Linux) or large software packages. For example, when you download Windows from Microsoft's site, you typically get an ISO file.

- **Creating a Bootable USB Drive:** An ISO image can be copied onto a USB drive to create a "bootable" USB drive. This means you can use this USB drive to boot your computer and install an operating system, as if you were using a CD or DVD.

  To create a bootable USB drive, you can use programs like Rufus or Etcher. These tools will copy the ISO image onto the USB drive and prepare it for booting the computer.

- **Direct Use of an ISO Image:** You can use an ISO image directly on your computer without burning it to a disc or putting it on a USB drive. Software like Daemon Tools or WinCDEmu allows you to "mount" an ISO image as if it were a disc inserted into a DVD drive.

How to Create or Use an ISO Image:

- **Downloading an ISO Image:** You can download ISO images, like those for operating systems, from official sites. For example, you can download the Windows 10 ISO image from Microsoft's website.

- **Creating a Bootable USB Drive:** Use a program like Rufus to copy the ISO image to a USB drive. This program will format the USB drive and transfer the files so that it can boot the computer.

- **Opening an ISO Image Directly:** On Windows 10 or 11, you can open an ISO image by right-clicking it and selecting "Mount." This allows you to view and use the files from the ISO as if they were on a CD or DVD.

Why Use an ISO Image?

- **Complete Backup:** An ISO image is

a convenient way to back up all the content of a disc, including important files and files necessary to start a computer.

- **Easy to Share:** An ISO file is easy to copy, share, or store on USB drives or hard disks.

- **Easy Emulation:** You can use an ISO image directly on your computer without needing to burn a physical disc, which is convenient and fast.

Creating a Bootable USB Drive:

1. **Using Software to Create a Bootable USB Drive:**

   Rufus (Windows) or Etcher (Multi-platform) are popular tools for creating a bootable USB drive.

   - **Insert a USB Drive:** Insert a USB drive with at least 8 GB capacity into your computer.
   - **Launch Rufus or Etcher:** Open the software and select the ISO image you downloaded.
   - **Select the USB Drive:** Choose the USB drive as the destination device.
   - **Click "Start":** Click "Start" to create the bootable USB drive. This process will erase everything on the USB drive, so make sure it does not contain important data.

2. **Configure the BIOS to Boot from the USB Drive:**

   - **Access the BIOS:** Restart your PC and enter the BIOS by pressing the appropriate key (often "Delete", "F2", or "Esc").

- **Change Boot Order:** In the BIOS, find the "Boot" menu and set the USB drive as the first device in the boot order. This will allow your PC to boot from the USB drive and begin the OS installation.

Installing the Operating System and Drivers

1. Install the Operating System:

Windows:

- When your PC boots from the USB drive, follow the on-screen instructions to install Windows. You will be prompted to enter your product key (if you have one) and select the disk where you want to install Windows.

Linux:

- For Linux, the process is similar. Follow the on-screen instructions to select the disk and configure your partitioning (choose the automatic installation if you are unsure).

2. Configure Windows/Linux:

Configure Windows:

- After installation, Windows will guide you through the initial setup: creating a user account, connecting to the internet, etc. Windows Update will automatically handle downloading generic drivers.

Configure Linux:

- In Linux, the initial setup will allow you to create a user account, configure the network, and update the system.

3. Install Specific Drivers:

Windows:

- After installation, go to "Device Manager" to check that all hardware components (graphics card, network card, etc.) are recognized. If some drivers are missing, download them from the manufacturer's websites (NVIDIA, AMD, Intel, etc.).
- It is also recommended to visit the motherboard manufacturer's website to install the latest drivers for the chipset, network, audio, and other integrated components.

Linux:

- Most drivers are included in the Linux kernel. However, for certain graphics cards (like NVIDIA), you may need to install proprietary drivers for better performance. This is usually done through the software manager or system settings.

4. Update the OS and Drivers:

Windows:

- Once all drivers are installed, use Windows Update to check for and install the latest security and feature updates.

Linux:

- In Linux, use the command `sudo apt update && sudo apt upgrade` (for Ubuntu and derivatives) to ensure your system and drivers are up-to-date.

By following these steps, you will have successfully installed the operating system and necessary drivers, making your PC fully operational. You can now start using your new machine for work, gaming, or any other activities you had in mind when building your PC.

Troubleshooting and Tips

After assembling your PC and installing the operating system, issues may arise. If your PC does not start or you encounter other problems, do not panic. Here is a troubleshooting guide for common issues, along with tips and resources for further assistance.

What to Do if the PC Does Not Start:

1. Check Connections:

- **Power Supply:** Ensure the power supply is properly plugged into the wall outlet and the power switch is set to "On". Verify that all power cables (24-pin, 8-pin CPU, PCIe for GPU) are securely connected.
- **Motherboard:** Check if the motherboard is receiving power. The motherboard LEDs should light up when the power is connected. If not, recheck the power connections.
- **Power Button:** Ensure the power button cable is correctly connected to the appropriate header on the motherboard. It's easy to plug this cable into the wrong header,

preventing the PC from turning on.

2. BIOS Beeps and Error Codes:

- **BIOS Beeps:** If your PC emits a series of beeps after pressing the power button, it indicates a hardware issue. Consult the motherboard manual to decode the BIOS beeps and identify the problem (e.g., RAM, GPU, or CPU issue).

- **Black Screen or No Display:** If the PC seems to start (fans running, LEDs on) but there is no display, check that the graphics card is properly seated in the PCIe slot and the video cable is correctly connected to the monitor. Try a different port on the graphics card or a different cable if possible.

3. Reset BIOS:

- **Clear CMOS:** If the PC still does not start, try resetting the BIOS. This can be done using the CMOS reset jumper on the motherboard or by removing the CMOS battery for a few minutes before reinserting it. This will reset the BIOS settings to default.

Common Problems and Solutions:

1. **Startup Issues:**

   - **No Response When Pressing Power Button:** Check that the power supply is properly connected. If nothing happens, try a different power outlet or power cable.

   - **Endless Reboots or Crashes:** This may indicate an overheating problem. Ensure the CPU cooler is properly installed and all fans are working correctly. Check BIOS settings, particularly voltage and frequency settings if you have overclocked the CPU or RAM.

2. **Display Issues:**

   - **No Video Signal:** Check that the graphics card is properly connected and cables are correctly plugged in. Try starting the PC with a single RAM module or use the motherboard's integrated video output (if available) to test the display.

   - **Incorrect Resolution or Refresh Rate:** After installing the OS, ensure graphics drivers are updated.

Resolution or refresh rate issues can often be resolved by updating or reinstalling graphics drivers.

3. **Storage Issues:**

- **Hard Drive or SSD Not Detected:** Check SATA and power connections to the drives. Ensure cables are properly connected and try a different SATA port on the motherboard.
- **Check BIOS:** Go into the BIOS to verify that the drive is detected and set as a boot device if necessary.

4. **Memory (RAM) Issues:**

- **Beeping Indicating RAM Issues:** Ensure RAM modules are properly seated in the slots. Try starting the PC with one RAM module at a time, testing each module and slot separately to identify a potential failure.
- **PC Freezes or Crashes:** This could be due to a RAM issue or incorrect BIOS settings (such as a misconfigured XMP profile). Try resetting the BIOS to default settings and disabling XMP profiles to see if it

resolves the problem.

Additional Resources (Forums, Communities):

1. Forums and Help Communities:

- **Tom's Hardware:** A very active forum with sections dedicated to PC troubleshooting. You can ask specific questions and get answers from the community.
  - Tom's Hardware Forum
- **Reddit (r/buildapc and r/techsupport):** These subreddits are great for technical questions or advice on PC building. The community is welcoming and helpful for beginners.
  - r/buildapc
  - r/techsupport
- **Linus Tech Tips Forum:** Another excellent resource for PC troubleshooting. The community is very responsive and has many discussions on common issues.
  - Linus Tech Tips Forum

2. Tutorial Videos:

- **YouTube:** There are many YouTube

channels specializing in PC building and troubleshooting, such as Linus Tech Tips, JayzTwoCents, and Gamers Nexus. These channels offer detailed videos that can guide you through common problems.

- Linus Tech Tips
- JayzTwoCents
- Gamers Nexus

3. Manufacturer Support Sites:

- **Manufacturer Websites:** If you encounter specific issues with hardware (like the motherboard or graphics card), check the manufacturer's website for troubleshooting guides, driver updates, and technical support.

By following these tips and using the resources mentioned, you should be able to resolve most issues you encounter with your PC. If problems persist, don't hesitate to seek help from forums or contact the technical support of your hardware manufacturers. The key is to stay patient and methodical in your troubleshooting approach.

Optimisation des Performances de votre PC

Une fois que votre PC est assemblé et opérationnel, il est essentiel d'optimiser ses performances pour tirer le meilleur parti de votre matériel. Cela peut inclure l'overclocking du processeur (CPU) et de la carte graphique (GPU), l'ajustement des paramètres du BIOS, et l'utilisation de logiciels gratuits pour améliorer les performances. Voici un guide détaillé pour chaque aspect de l'optimisation.

1. Overclocking du CPU et du GPU

1.1 Overclocking du CPU

Comprendre l'Overclocking: L'overclocking consiste à augmenter la fréquence d'horloge du processeur au-delà de ses spécifications d'usine pour améliorer ses performances. Les processeurs Intel avec un suffixe "K" (comme les i5-13600K) et les processeurs AMD Ryzen sont généralement conçus pour être overclockés.

Accéder au BIOS pour Overclocker:

- **Redémarrez votre PC** et accédez au BIOS en appuyant sur la touche appropriée ("Delete", "F2", "Esc" selon le fabricant).
- **Recherchez les options d'overclocking**

dans le BIOS, souvent sous les menus "OC" (Overclocking) ou "Tweaker".

- **Augmentez progressivement le multiplicateur** du CPU. Par exemple, si votre CPU fonctionne à 3.6 GHz (36 x 100 MHz), essayez d'augmenter le multiplicateur à 37 pour obtenir 3.7 GHz.

Tester la Stabilité:

- **Enregistrez les modifications** dans le BIOS et redémarrez le PC.
- **Utilisez des logiciels de test de stabilité** comme Prime95 ou AIDA64 pour vérifier la stabilité sous charge. Si des instabilités ou des erreurs apparaissent, revenez au BIOS pour réduire légèrement l'overclock ou augmenter la tension du CPU avec prudence.

Surveiller les Températures:

- **Utilisez des logiciels** comme HWMonitor ou Core Temp pour surveiller les températures du CPU. Si le CPU dépasse 85°C sous charge, ajustez l'overclock ou améliorez le refroidissement pour éviter des dommages à long terme.

1.2 Overclocking du GPU

Utiliser des Logiciels d'Overclocking:

- **MSI Afterburner** et **EVGA Precision X1** sont des outils populaires pour overclocker votre carte graphique. Ils permettent de modifier la fréquence d'horloge du GPU, la vitesse de la mémoire, et de contrôler la courbe de ventilation.

Augmenter la Fréquence du GPU:

- **Commencez par augmenter légèrement** la fréquence d'horloge du GPU par incréments de 10-20 MHz. Testez la stabilité avec des outils comme 3DMark ou Unigine Heaven.
- **Continuez à augmenter** jusqu'à ce que vous atteigniez la limite de stabilité.

Optimiser les Paramètres de la Mémoire:

- **Augmentez progressivement** la fréquence de la mémoire vidéo (VRAM) pour améliorer les performances graphiques. Les gains peuvent être notables dans les jeux ou les applications 3D.

Surveiller la Température et la Stabilité:

- **Utilisez MSI Afterburner** pour surveiller les températures du GPU pendant

189

l'overclocking. Veillez à ce que les températures restent en dessous de 85°C pour éviter des dommages potentiels.

2. Optimisation du BIOS et des Paramètres Système

2.1 Optimisation du BIOS

Activer le XMP pour la RAM:

- **Activez le profil XMP (Extreme Memory Profile)** dans le BIOS pour faire fonctionner votre RAM à sa fréquence maximale spécifiée. Cela permet à votre RAM de fonctionner à des vitesses plus élevées que celles par défaut.

Ajuster les Paramètres d'Alimentation:

- **Configurez les paramètres d'alimentation** pour optimiser les performances, par exemple en activant le "Performance Mode" ou "High Performance" pour assurer que le CPU fonctionne à pleine capacité lorsque nécessaire.

Configurer l'Ordre de Démarrage:

- **Assurez-vous que le disque principal** (où le système d'exploitation est installé) est configuré comme premier périphérique de démarrage pour accélérer le démarrage du PC.

2.2 Optimisation des Paramètres Système

Configurer Windows pour les Performances:

- **Accédez aux paramètres de Windows** : Allez dans "Système" > "Alimentation et mise en veille" > "Paramètres d'alimentation supplémentaires". Sélectionnez "Haute performance" pour garantir que le système utilise toute la puissance disponible.
- **Désactivez les effets visuels inutiles** : Accédez à "Système" > "Paramètres avancés du système" > "Paramètres de performance" et choisissez "Ajuster pour obtenir les meilleures performances" pour désactiver les animations et effets visuels non nécessaires.

Mettre à Jour les Pilotes:

- **Assurez-vous que tous les pilotes** de votre système sont à jour, en particulier ceux du GPU et du chipset. Les pilotes à jour peuvent offrir des optimisations de performance et résoudre des problèmes de compatibilité.

3. Logiciels Gratuits pour Booster les Performances

3.1 Utilitaires de Nettoyage Système

CCleaner:

- **Nettoyez les fichiers temporaires**, gérez les programmes au démarrage et réparez les erreurs de registre avec CCleaner. Un système propre et bien entretenu fonctionne généralement de manière plus fluide.

Defraggler (pour les HDD):

- **Défragmentez les disques durs (HDD)** avec Defraggler pour améliorer les temps d'accès aux fichiers. La défragmentation n'est pas nécessaire pour les SSD.

3.2 Gestion de la Mémoire et des Programmes

RAMMap:

- **Visualisez et gérez l'utilisation de la mémoire** avec RAMMap. Cet utilitaire de Microsoft est utile pour identifier les programmes gourmands en mémoire et libérer des ressources.

Autoruns:

- **Gérez les programmes au démarrage** avec Autoruns. Ce logiciel de Microsoft vous permet de voir et de désactiver les programmes qui démarrent avec Windows, ce qui peut accélérer le démarrage de votre PC et libérer des ressources.

3.3 Optimisation des Jeux Vidéo

Razer Cortex:

- **Optimisez les performances de votre PC pour les jeux** avec Razer Cortex. Ce logiciel ferme automatiquement les processus non essentiels et libère des ressources système, ce qui peut améliorer les FPS (images par seconde) dans les jeux exigeants.

NVIDIA GeForce Experience / AMD Radeon Software:

- **Optimisez automatiquement les paramètres de vos jeux** et mettez à jour les pilotes graphiques avec les outils fournis par les fabricants de GPU. Ces logiciels ajustent les paramètres pour obtenir les meilleures performances en fonction de votre matériel.

En utilisant ces techniques et outils, vous pouvez

193

maximiser les performances de votre PC sans frais supplémentaires. L'overclocking et l'optimisation des paramètres système peuvent considérablement améliorer la performance, en particulier pour les jeux et les applications exigeantes. Veillez à surveiller régulièrement votre système pour garantir qu'il fonctionne à son plein potentiel tout en restant stable et fiable.

15. Conclusion

Now that you've assembled and optimized your PC, it's important to think about regular maintenance and updates to ensure its longevity and performance. Here are some tips for maintaining your PC, updating its components over time, and considering future upgrades.

Maintaining Your PC

1. Regular Cleaning

Cleaning the Inside of the Case: Dust can accumulate quickly inside your case, reducing cooling efficiency and raising component temperatures. It's recommended to clean the inside of your PC every three to six months. Use compressed air to blow dust off fans, the CPU heatsink, dust filters, and corners of the case. Make sure to do this in a well-ventilated area.

Cleaning Peripherals: Your keyboard, mouse, and monitor can also collect dust and fingerprints. Clean them regularly with a soft, dry cloth or slightly dampened for dirtier surfaces.

2. Software Updates

Operating System Updates: Ensure your

operating system is always up to date with the latest security patches and new features. This not only ensures security but also compatibility with new software and games.

Driver Updates: Drivers, particularly for the graphics card and motherboard chipset, should be updated regularly to optimize performance and resolve potential issues. Use tools provided by manufacturers, such as GeForce Experience for NVIDIA cards or Radeon Software for AMD cards.

3. Checking Component Health

Monitoring Temperatures: Use software such as HWMonitor or Core Temp to regularly monitor the temperatures of your CPU, GPU, and other critical components. Consistently high temperatures may indicate a cooling problem that needs addressing.

Checking Disk Health: Use tools like CrystalDiskInfo to monitor the health of your hard drives and SSDs. This tool will alert you if a disk shows signs of imminent failure, giving you time to back up your data and replace the drive if necessary.

Updating Components

1. When and Why to Upgrade

Increasing Performance Needs: If your performance needs are increasing (e.g., for newer games or more demanding creative software), it might be time to upgrade components like the GPU or add more RAM.

Technological Obsolescence: Technology evolves rapidly, and some components may become outdated after a few years. For example, older CPUs or GPUs may limit your system's performance with newer software or games.

Storage Upgrades: If you're running out of storage space or want faster solutions, consider adding an extra SSD or replacing an HDD with an SSD.

2. Components to Update

Graphics Card (GPU): The GPU is often one of the first components to be updated, especially for gamers or content creators. A new graphics card can provide significantly improved graphical performance.

RAM: Adding more RAM or upgrading to faster modules can enhance overall performance, particularly for multitasking or memory-intensive applications.

Processor (CPU): If you're still using a several-generation-old processor, an upgrade can offer a significant performance boost, especially for CPU-intensive tasks like video editing or 3D rendering.

Cooling: If you decide to overclock further or if your system is running too hot, upgrading your cooling system (such as switching to liquid cooling or adding additional fans) may be necessary.

Tips for Future Upgrades

1. Planning for Upgrades

Compatibility: Before purchasing a new component, ensure it's compatible with your existing motherboard and power supply. For example, a new, more powerful graphics card may require a higher wattage power supply or additional connectors.

Future-Proofing: When upgrading a component, consider future needs. For instance, choosing a more powerful power supply from the start can make future upgrades easier without needing to replace the PSU every time.

Keeping Up with New Technologies: Stay informed about new technologies and upcoming product releases. Sometimes, waiting a few months for a new generation of components can offer better performance for a similar price.

2. Balancing Budget and Performance

Best Value for Money: Don't always seek the most expensive or latest component. Sometimes, a model from the previous generation offers a better price-to-performance ratio while meeting your needs.

Avoid Over-Spending: Upgrade components based on your actual needs. For example, if you only game occasionally or don't use highly demanding applications, a mid-range GPU may suffice, even if high-end models are available.

3. Considering New Accessories

Peripherals: As you upgrade internal components, also think about peripherals. A new gaming mouse, mechanical keyboard, or monitor with a higher refresh rate can also enhance your overall user experience.

By following these tips for maintenance, updates, and future upgrades, you ensure that your PC remains in top condition and continues to deliver high performance over the years. A well-maintained and regularly updated PC can provide excellent performance for many years, allowing you to fully enjoy your initial investment.

Appendices

Glossary of Technical Terms

- **BIOS (Basic Input/Output System):** Low-level software that initializes the computer's hardware components during startup and provides access to system settings.
- **CPU (Central Processing Unit):** The main processor of the computer that executes software instructions and manages everyday tasks.
- **GPU (Graphics Processing Unit):** A processor dedicated to rendering graphics, primarily used for gaming, video editing, and 3D applications.
- **RAM (Random Access Memory):** Volatile memory used to temporarily store data for programs currently in use, allowing for quick access.

- **SSD (Solid State Drive):** A storage drive using flash memory, faster than traditional hard drives (HDD), used for storing the operating system and important files.
- **PSU (Power Supply Unit):** The component that provides power to all of the computer's components.
- **Overclocking:** The process of increasing the CPU or GPU clock frequency beyond factory specifications to boost performance.
- **XMP (Extreme Memory Profile):** A memory profile that allows automatic overclocking of RAM to its maximum supported speed.
- **SATA (Serial ATA):** An interface used to connect hard drives and SSDs to the motherboard.
- **PCIe (Peripheral Component Interconnect Express):** A fast interface used to connect components such as graphics cards, NVMe SSDs, and other expansion cards to the motherboard.
- **CMOS (Complementary Metal-Oxide Semiconductor):** Technology used for small batteries on the motherboard that power the BIOS when the computer is off, maintaining configuration settings.

- **Thermal Throttling:** Automatic reduction in CPU or GPU speed to prevent overheating, usually due to inadequate cooling.

Final Check-list Before Startup

1. Preparation and Assembly

- All components are correctly installed (CPU, RAM, GPU, SSD/HDD, PSU).
- The case is well-organized with proper cable management for optimal airflow.
- Fans are correctly oriented for intake and exhaust.
- Thermal paste is applied (if needed) and the cooling system is securely mounted.

2. Connections

- The 24-pin power cable is connected to the motherboard.
- The CPU power cable (8 or 4 pins) is connected near the processor.
- PCIe power cables are connected to the graphics card.
- Hard drives and SSDs are connected with SATA cables (data and power).

- Fan cables are connected to the appropriate headers on the motherboard.

3. Initial Checks

- The PC is plugged into a functional power outlet.
- The monitor is connected to the graphics card's video output and powered on.
- The keyboard and mouse are connected to USB ports.

4. First Startup

- The power button is correctly connected and functioning.
- The PC starts up without error beeps (or with the correct number of beeps) and displays the BIOS.
- All components (RAM, CPU, GPU, SSD/HDD) are detected in the BIOS.
- Component temperatures are within normal ranges in the BIOS.

5. Operating System Installation

- The bootable USB drive with the OS is ready and selected as the first boot device.

- The operating system installs without errors.
- Drivers are installed after the OS installation.

6. **Finalization**

- All monitoring software (for temperature, overclocking, etc.) is installed.
- The PC is stable after several hours of operation.
- All Windows/Linux and driver updates are installed.

This appendix completes the guide and serves as a quick reference for technical terms, component comparisons, and a checklist to ensure your PC is ready for use. Following these steps guarantees a successful installation and a confident startup of your new PC.

www.ingramcontent.com/pod-product-compliance
Lightning Source LLC
Chambersburg PA
CBHW052140070326
40690CB00047B/1251